For Carolyn Choa

MADE IN BANGKOK

Made in Bangkok was first performed at the Aldwych Theatre, London, in March 1986 with Felicity Kendal and Peter McEnery in a Michael Codron production directed by Michael Blakemore.

'As its title might suggest, *Made in Bangkok* is about trade and sex: of the five British we follow from airport through factory to brothel only Frances, the wife of a sadistic British executive, has not come East to exploit the natives, either physically or commercially . . . The best new English play since *Benefactors*, it asks all the right questions about human exploitation, while managing also to be a bittersweet comedy about impossible sexual differences.' Sheridan Morley, *Punch*

'Under a deceptively comic surface, Anthony Minghella's play offers a dark and troubled view of both Eastern and Western values. Mr Minghella reminds me very much of Peter Nichols in his lightning switches of mood and, at a time when one begins to despair of young writers fulfilling early Fringe promise, it shows him commanding a West End stage with great accomplishment.' Michael Billington, *Guardian*

'An extremely funny play but also a scathing indictment of our so-called civilised society.'
Jane Edwardes, *Time Out*

'Strong, brave, uncomfortable, provocative stuff.' Lyn Gardner, *City Limits*

Anthony Minghella was born in 1954 on the Isle of Wight of Italian parents. Until 1981 he taught at the University of Hull, and since then he has written for the stage, television and radio. His plays include *Child's Play, Whale Music, A Little Like Drowning, Two Planks and a Passion, Love Bites* and a television trilogy, *What If It's Raining? Made in Bangkok* is his first play since winning the Theatre Critics' Award for Most Promising Playwright of 1984. It was commissioned by Michael Codron.

The front cover shows a stucco frieze of walking monks at Wat Mahathat in the ancient city of Sukhothai in Thailand. The photograph appears in the 'Insight Guide to Thailand' and is reproduced by courtesy of APA Productions (HK) Ltd.

GW00691574

A METHUEN THEATRESCRIPT

First published in Great Britain in 1986 as a paperback original by Methuen London Ltd, 11 New Fetter Lane, London EC4P 4EE and in the United States of America by Methuen Inc, 29 West 35th Street, New York, NY 10001.

Copyright © 1986 by Anthony Minghella

Acknowledgement
The lines from the *Insight Guide to Thailand* quoted on page 7 are reprinted by kind permission of Apa Productions (HK) Ltd.

British Library Cataloguing in Publication Data:

Minghella, Anthony
    Made in Bangkok.
    I. Title
    822'.914   PR 6063.I4/

    ISBN 0-413-42410-3

Set and printed in Great Britain by Expression Printers Ltd, London N7

MADE IN BANGKOK

ANTHONY MINGHELLA

A Methuen Paperback

Made in Bangkok was first presented in London at the Aldwych Theatre on 18 March 1986 by Michael Codron. It had the following cast:

ADRIAN WEST, *owner of a chain of boutiques*	Benjamin Whitrow
GARY ALEXANDER, *his assistant, early 20s*	Christopher Fulford
STEPHEN BRITTER, *a junior executive of a multinational computer firm, early 30s*	Paul Shelley
FRANCES BRITTER, *reviews books, would like to write them, Stephen's wife, early 30s*	Felicity Kendal
EDWARD GOVER, *a dentist working for WHO in Hong Kong, mid-30s*	Peter McEnery
NET, *a hotel worker*	David Yip
COURIER ⎱ MRS LWIN ⎰	Diana Choy
THAI GIRL	Leanne Hong
THAI GIRL	Tia Lee
THAI GIRL ⎱ AMPHA ⎰	Susan Tan
FACTORY OWNER ⎱ MR LWIN ⎰	Vincent Wong
ARMY OFFICER ⎱ MASSAGE PARLOUR PROPRIETOR ⎰	Eddie Yeoh

Directed by Michael Blakemore
Designed by John Gunter
Lighting designed by David Hersey
Costumes designed by Diane Holmes

Scene: the place is Bangkok, Thailand. The time is now.

ACT ONE

Scene One

*Don Muang airport. Bangkok. Thailand.
5 a.m. Baggage reclaiming area. A
carousel with a single suitcase revolving.
Somewhere, perhaps, a flight number
indicating that this is the location for
passenger baggage arriving on a Thai
international flight from London,
Heathrow.*

*A small group of travellers remain at the
carousel. They are all part of the same tour,
'Eastern Promise' Tours. They have
evidently been waiting for some time. Each
couple, and EDWARD, have luggage
trolleys to the ready. Their handluggage is
labelled with 'Eastern Promise' tags.
FRANCES is reading avidly, sitting on her
trolley, STEPHEN is temporarily absent.*

GARY: This is a joke, isn't it? (*He pulls off
his shirt and drapes it over the trolley, then
loudly and drawing attention to himself:*)
Excuse me, but we are rather struggling
over here on the luggage front.

EDWARD: I think you'll find – we're all
with the same tour – that our bags are held
up for some reason.

GARY: Give the man a medal.

EDWARD: No, I'm just pointing out . . .

GARY: We had deduced that ourselves,
that we are all standing by this conveyor
belt because our luggage hasn't turned
up.

ADRIAN: Shut up Gary.

GARY (*to* ADRIAN): Apart from
anything else I've had a hard-on since
Heathrow.

STEPHEN *enters.*

STEPHEN: Outside, apparently, it's 103
degrees. And raining.

FRANCES: What did they say?

STEPHEN: I don't know. Nothing.
Everything's closed. The chap over there
pointed back over here and I said we
knew that.

FRANCES: We should ring the hotel.

STEPHEN: I haven't got coins.

FRANCES: Well surely the . . .

STEPHEN: Yes, all right, I have been on a
plane for practically a year.

FRANCES: I just thought . . .

STEPHEN: Inevitably, as soon as I get
through the luggage will arrive or the
courier, the tour operator, the rep,
whoever, and – (*In a hugely irritated
gesture he pulls the suitcase off the
carousel.*) – I'm sorry but I can't just
watch this thing lurch round. Is it
anybody's?

GARY (*of* EDWARD): Ask Mastermind.

EDWARD (*to* GARY *who's smoking*): It
does say no smoking. It's bad enough as it
is without the fug to contend with.

GARY: Oh, the fug!

EDWARD (*intimidated*): I'm going to find
out . . . (*Picks up the suitcase.*) Is this
anybody's? (*It's heavy. He puts it down
and exits weakly.*)

GARY: Wanker.

ADRIAN: Go away, Gary, will you.

GARY'S *attention is caught by some signs
in Thai, a flowing secret script, all dashes
and undulations.*

GARY: Have you seen this, the writing,
joke eh? Do you reckon it actually means
anything?

ADRIAN: Oh, I doubt it.

GARY: Is it advertising women? This is the
question.

*He settles down with his walkman, which
is playing loud rock music. He jigs
occasionally to its hidden beat.*

FRANCES: (*reading from her 'Insight
Guide to Thailand'*): I'm glad Katie
recommended this. (*The book.*) It is
good. Quite vivid.

STEPHEN (*of the wait*): This is a farce.

GARY *sings noisily and tunelessly along
with the song on his headphones.*

STEPHEN (*to* ADRIAN): Are you going
on to Hong Kong?

ADRIAN: Yes.

STEPHEN: Yes. And what, Eastern
Promise Tours?

ADRIAN: Yes.

STEPHEN: Us too. (*Of the wait:*) Not the
best of starts.

ADRIAN: No.

STEPHEN: We'd understood the courier, the rep would be here.

ADRIAN: Right.

STEPHEN: It's typical.

ADRIAN: Why? Do you know Bangkok?

STEPHEN: No. I suppose I meant . . .

FRANCES: This is good. It describes Thailand as an arm with Burma as its epaulette and Malaysia as its glove. Very military. (*She looks up.*)

STEPHEN: This is my wife, Francis.

ADRIAN: Hello.

STEPHEN: I'm Stephen.

GARY (*slipping his headphones and addressing* ADRIAN): Talking to me?

ADRIAN: No.

FRANCES: Is Cambodia the same as Kampuchea? I'm embarrassed to ask.

STEPHEN *doesn't know.*

STEPHEN: What?

ADRIAN: Yes.

Then EDWARD *returns followed by a Thai* ARMY OFFICER.

OFFICER (*to the assembled*): I am sorry for this problem.

EDWARD (*confidently*): Apparently the Royal Family are driving out of Bangkok this morning and the roads have been cleared, which explains the . . .

STEPHEN: What about our luggage?

OFFICER: A slight delay. (*Smiles.*)

ADRIAN: A long delay.

OFFICER: We are cursed in our country with the problem of drugs. We have to be most scrupulous.

STEPHEN: What, and you think we're bringing in drugs?

ADRIAN: I thought the problem was drugs going out.

OFFICER: As I say: there is no problem and your luggage will be with you in a few moments.

EDWARD (*pointedly, in* GARY's direction): Clearly some of us look like drug pushers.

GARY (*slipping his headphones*): What's going on? Coup, is it?

ADRIAN: Apparently some of us look like we're on drugs.

GARY: Oh yeah? Terrific. (*Back to walkman.*)

STEPHEN (*irritated, to the* ARMY OFFICER): It's just we have actually been flying all night.

Two Thai girls appear, very respectable and conservatively dressed. They have a baggage trolley. They aim for the stranded suitcase. It's very heavy. GARY *springs to his feet.*

GARY (*helping them*): There you go. All right?

The girls smile their thanks and make to leave.

(*To them:*) Speak English? Eh? (*Then mischievously, at a safe distance:*) I suppose a fuck's out of the question?

The girls steer their trolley away.

EDWARD (*to the* ARMY OFFICER *et al*): We were wondering whose that was. The suitcase.

OFFICER: Very pretty girls, eh?

GARY: Brilliant.

OFFICER: Patpong I! Good!

STEPHEN: Patpong? So they say.

FRANCES: What's that?

OFFICER (*to* EDWARD): You like nice Thai girls?

EDWARD: What? Yes. I mean I like the Thai people. I speak some Thai actually.

OFFICER: Oh yes?

EDWARD: Mai pen rai. Obviously. And Kawpkun. Sabmidi Kawpkun.

OFFICER (*correct pronunciation*): Kawpkun. Very good.

EDWARD: I mean obviously I'm not fluent. My Cantonese is quite good. And I can manage a few words in Vietnamese. I'm not a linguist. I'm a dentist.

OFFICER: Ah.

EDWARD: Yes, as a matter of fact I work in the Vietnamese Refugee Camps in Hong Kong. Do you know who I mean?

The Boat People?

OFFICER: For the Thai . . . Vietnam . . .
(*Shrugs.*) We argue like brother and
sister. Very close, very big arguments.

FRANCES (*now reading again*): The South
sounds amazing. And the North.
Unspoiled.

EDWARD: That's right, because many of
these people speak of having run the
gauntlet of Thai pirates before reaching
Hong Kong.

FRANCES (*reading*): Bangkok, though, is
sinking. Apparently.

OFFICER: What do you mean, Thai
pirates?

EDWARD: Obviously not ordinary, and
now they have to live like prisoners in
these camps in HK, like rats . . .
the hygiene is . . . ach! No, of course,
most Thai people are terribly friendly.

OFFICER: We smile all the time.

EDWARD: Yes. Marvellous teeth.

OFFICER: So you come to Bangkok meet
nice Thai girl?

EDWARD: Well . . .

FRANCES (*reading*): God! Stephen . . .
Listen to this . . . 'A less well-known
shrine in Bangkok, but highly regarded
by its followers, consists entirely of erect
phalluses, from the small to the
gargantuan, sculpted from wood, wax,
stone, cement, with scrupulous fidelity to
life.' God! Typical. Talk about self-
worship.

STEPHEN: I don't particularly want to talk
about anything. I'd like our luggage to
arrive and a car to the hotel and then a
sleep.

FRANCES: We can't sleep now. It's
morning.

STEPHEN: Nevertheless.

The carousel suddenly lurches to a halt.

GARY (*sarcastic*): Brilliant.

STEPHEN: Now what?

OFFICER: If you would excuse me. I will
investigate.

*He exits, talking sharply into a crackling
walkie-talkie.*

GARY (*to* EDWARD): Nice chat?

EDWARD: I hope you're not carrying
drugs.

GARY: Don't worry, they're up my arse.

ADRIAN: It's not drugs . . . I expect it's just
military paranoia. They go in for it these
days. It's like landing at an Army Base,
not an airport.

STEPHEN: That's right. Probably think
we've got a bomb or something.

EDWARD: Could be my fault. I'm
politically quite, you know: I get various
journals.

GARY: Eh up, it's Arthur Scargill.

FRANCES: They wouldn't think of
building a shrine of vaginas.

STEPHEN: It would be a bit odd, wouldn't
it?

FRANCES: Why?

STEPHEN: There's no need to shout.

FRANCES: I'm not shouting. Why would
vaginas be odd?

STEPHEN: What do they look like for
God's sake? It's what they're not rather
than what they are, isn't it?

FRANCIS: Is it? Oh, I see.

STEPHEN: You might at least have the
good grace to concede that the one is an
accepted symbol and the other is not.
There are not to my knowledge any
leaning Holes of Pisa . . . the Eiffel
Hole . . .

FRANCES: I think that was my point.

STEPHEN: Well then, Frances: you win.

NET *and the female*
REPRESENTATIVE *from Eastern
Promise Tours arrive.* NET *works for the
hotel. The* EP REPRESENTATIVE
wears a sash with the company logo.

EDWARD: Ah, finally.

REP: So sorry. Good morning. Welcome to
Bangkok. No baggage yet? (*Quite cool
and collected. She consults her clipboard.*)
Mr, Mrs Britter?

STEPHEN: That's right. No. No baggage
yet.

REP (*to them*): Room 202. (*Then to*

ADRIAN *and* GARY:) Mr West. Mr. Alexander.

ADRIAN: Yes.

GARY (*from inside the walkman*): Ah, is this action on the action front?

REP: Room 203. (*Looks to* EDWARD, *mispronounces his surname:*) Mr Gover?

EDWARD (*correcting her*): Gover, yes.

REP: Room 205 –

GARY (*interrupting*): Excuse me, there are two of us.

The REPRESENTATIVE *shrugs.*

GARY: And we're not going out with each other.

REP (*consulting list*): This was our booking detail. You must check at hotel.

ADRIAN: Don't worry. We'll sort it out.

GARY (*of sharing a room*): Fuck that for a game of soldiers.

EDWARD: We're all rather aggravated about this luggage business.

REP: I will ask about the delay.

EDWARD: It's not as if we're a party or anything, so why we should all have to wait simply because we booked through the same company –

EDWARD *is interrupted by the renaissance of the baggage carousel.*

STEPHEN (*arch*): Hurray.

The first luggage belongs to ADRIAN *and* GARY.

GARY (*at the carousel*): OK, let's go.

NET: No problem. (*Helping* GARY *load the trolley.*) Net help.

FRANCES: These are ours, Stephen.

STEPHEN: Yes OK.

REP (*of* NET): This man will drive us to the hotel.

EDWARD: Where are mine?

A case appears.

Well, that's one . . . but there's a large package, a . . . now what's happened?

GARY (*ready*): Where do we go?

NET: This way.

REP: Just wait for Mr Gover.

GARY: Why? (*Mimicking:*) Just because we're in the same party? Come on.

EDWARD *watches the carousel with increasing impatience.*

EDWARD: This really is . . . (*Snorts:*) . . . Ach! How can one bag just . . .

REP: Expect just coming.

EDWARD (*arch*): Do you?

STEPHEN: Well . . . there's clearly some sort of problem with your bag which is probably why we've had to . . .

EDWARD: I don't see why you . . .

STEPHEN (*to* ADRIAN): I mean, it must be.

FRANCES: It doesn't matter. We can wait. Stephen?

STEPHEN: We don't seem to have much . . .

GARY: Why do we have to hang around waiting for Arthur? It's not a school outing.

ADRIAN: Then grow up. No actually just shut up.

EDWARD: Thank you.

Along comes EDWARD's *parcel . . . bustling down the chute on to the carousel. It's a brown paper sack, like a potato sack, which has been taped and strung, but clearly opened. As it makes its entry, to* EDWARD's *relief and other weary grunts, it spills its contents all over the floor. Hundreds of toothbrushes.*

EDWARD: Sod it! Buggeration! Sod it!

GARY (*picking one up*): Aye-Aye! He's smuggling in toothbrushes.

EDWARD: Yes, well I'm a dentist. (*Scrabbling to pick them up.*)

GARY: A likely story, Arthur.

EDWARD: This parcel has been deliberately . . . (*As he picks it up the remainder of the brushes scatter.*) Sod it!

NET (*helping*): No problem.

REP: Best thing, Net help you pack bag. I take other guests to minibus. This way please.

FRANCES: Well, I'm sure we can . . .

STEPHEN (*as he exits*): Fran . . .

FRANCES (*sympathetically to* EDWARD): Well, good luck.

She leaves, leaving NET *and* EDWARD *alone, retrieving toothbrushes.*

EDWARD: Thanks for . . .

NET: No problem.

EDWARD: I didn't, did you say your name?

NET: Net.

EDWARD: I'm Edward.

NET (*of the toothbrushes and the events*): Army. Very suspicious. Very powerful.

EDWARD: Right.

NET: Edward dentist?

EDWARD: That's right.

NET: I have very bad mouth all night.(*Opens mouth.*) Big pain.

EDWARD: I can't look at your teeth at the minute.

NET: How much you want?

EDWARD: No it's not, it's just . . .

NET: No problem. Finish here. Net take Mr Edward to hotel room. Come up later for teeth.

EDWARD: I don't . . . really, I'm on . . .

NET: Net understand. No problem. You Bangkok business or pleasure?

EDWARD: Uh . . .

NET: Half-half?

EDWARD: Tourist.

NET: You have wife? Girlfriend?

EDWARD: No. Not at the minute.

NET: Net find Edward nice girl.

EDWARD: I don't think so.

NET: Funny. Everybody come to Bangkok say no girl, no girl. Later they ask Net find nice girl.

EDWARD: Right. I'll remember.

NET: Everybody say no at first. If Edward embarrassed I can have girl come to room. Very private. Talking 1,000 baht.

EDWARD (*saying no*): Really.

NET: Eight hundred. Special price. Eight hundred. Yes or no?

EDWARD: No thank you. I don't want a girlfriend.

NET (*hot on colloquialism*): There you go. (*As they complete the collection of the toothbrushes.*)

EDWARD: Ta. Good. I'll have to just try and (*As he struggles to repair the sack in some way.*) Bloody thing. (*A brush slips out again.* EDWARD *gives it to* NET.) Have it, go on.

NET: For me?

EDWARD: Well don't worry. I've got plenty. Hundreds

NET: Thank you. Edward kind man.

EDWARD: No. Anyway, they're for the refugees. In Hong Kong. I look after their teeth. So they're not for sale or anything. (*Wearily but thawing:*) Anyway, come on. Let me see. Open your mouth.

NET *obliges instantly. His mouth wide open.*

Which one is causing the problem? Here? (NET *groans in acknowledgement.*) Yes. Well, I can't say I'm surprised. Do you brush your teeth after you've eaten? Hm? You see, you've still got your wisdom tooth there haven't you? Up top? You haven't been getting around it. I think you're going to need that looking at. Do you use floss?

NET (*now able to talk for the first time as* EDWARD *cleans his hands on a handkerchief*): Up here hurts. Sometimes blood in mouth.

EDWARD: Well yes, you're infected, your gums are sore, you've got great build-up of plaque, and you smoke too much, your teeth are all stained, and you need some filling work. Go to a dentist. When I'm unpacked I'll give you some Oil of Cloves . . . Remind me. It's nothing fancy, but it'll ease the pain if you rub it into your gum.

NET: Rub in . . . (NET *copies* EDWARD.) No kid?

EDWARD: No kid. And I've probably got a mouthwash: Bocasin or something. If it hasn't been . . . (*referring sulkily to his luggage.*) Anyway, we'll sort you out.

NET (*as he stacks the parcel on to the trolley*): Hundreds of toothbrush. (*Impressed*:) Fa!

EDWARD: So.

NET: We go now.

EDWARD: Right.

NET: OK, before my friend leave Bangkok, Net make sure he has good time.

EDWARD: OK. Listen, have a toothbrush for your wife.

NET: No. No problem. We share, thank you. OK, let's go.

They exit, pushing off the trolley.

Scene Two

GARY *and* ADRIAN's *room.* GARY *is disgruntled with the sleeping arrangements.*

GARY: And they're not even double beds.

ADRIAN: You'll live. It's only for a few days.

GARY: A very important few days.

ADRIAN: If you're so anxious you can book into another hotel.

GARY: I might. I told you the geezer on Reception said he could fix us up, no bother?

ADRIAN: I'm sure he did.

GARY: Well.

ADRIAN: Look. Let me tell you something about this place . . . if you want to piss all over a woman in Bangkok you can, if you can pay for it, and you don't have to pay much.

GARY: Who wants to piss all over a woman?

ADRIAN: You'd be surprised.

GARY: He said these girls were really fresh, from up country, young and – you know – not . . .

ADRIAN: Listen Gary, you do whatever you want. Just turn up to our appointments and don't fornicate in my bed.

GARY: Fair dos.

ADRIAN: In fact, don't fornicate in your own bed when I'm in my bed. I might get embarrassed.

GARY: I'll get you lots of brochures for guided tours. Fancy a long walk this afternoon?

ADRIAN: I fancy a long sleep.

GARY: What you doing?

ADRIAN: Checking the sheets. I don't want to lie in somebody else's sweat.

GARY: My shirt's gone dry now. (*Taking it off.*)

ADRIAN: Do you think this is a clean sheet? Probably not. It's probably like your shirt.

GARY: 'Cause you look out of the window, it looks like nothing, the weather looks like London practically, but outside it's a real bastard.

ADRIAN: You haven't been outside. I'm going to have these sheets changed.

GARY: At the airport. You know what I mean.

ADRIAN: Don't behave like a prat while we're here, Gary. I brought you along to learn some things, learn some business. Be grateful. Don't be a prat, eh? (*To the phone*:) Hello. Hello. Room service?

GARY: What do you mean?

ADRIAN: You were a prat on the plane. And at the airport.

GARY: I was bored.

ADRIAN: You were boring. And pissed . . . (*To the phone*:) Yes, I'm in Room – Is that room service? – Yes, I'm in Room 203, yes, 203. I'd like the linen changed on the beds please. The sheets. (*Pause.*) Because they're not clean. (*Pause.*) That's what I said. No, I just want them changed. Thank you. (*To* GARY:) Because I haven't got the patience.

GARY: What do I do before the night life?

ADRIAN: There was a lizard in the bathroom. You could warm up on that.

GARY: There's a coffee shop with a juke box. What time do you think that gets going?

ADRIAN: You're serious, aren't you?

GARY: I didn't come for the food poisoning.

ADRIAN: What did you come for?

GARY: Now you're being serious.

ADRIAN: Well?

GARY: To help you find a factory.

ADRIAN: Go on.

GARY: I've got a good eye. I know what will sell. I can tell the difference between . . .

ADRIAN: No, why else did you come?

GARY: To fuck. You can't embarrass me.

ADRIAN: Why?

GARY: I like it.

ADRIAN: But why here in particular?

GARY: No I always like it. Here it's cheap. Why did we come here for clothes? Good stuff: good price. No one asks too many questions. I told you you can't phase me.

ADRIAN: And what are you looking for? What turns you on?

GARY: Fuck off.

ADRIAN: No, I'm interested. (*Knock on the door. To the knocker*:) Just a minute.

It's the maids, two of them, come to deal with the sheets. They walk straight in. They begin to change the linen on GARY's *bed.*

GARY: Don't mind us.

ADRIAN: It's the other bed I want changing.

GARY: We could have been doing anything. Just walking straight in!

ADRIAN: You think they haven't seen it before?

GARY: Not mine, love.

ADRIAN: Where were we? Oh yes. What about these two? Any use?

GARY: Don't fancy yours.

ADRIAN: I'm still serious.

GARY: Don't fancy yours.

ADRIAN: Shall I ask? Save you the bother of going downstairs.

GARY: I know you're just winding me up.

ADRIAN: Now I'm confused. You came here for some women. Here are some women. What's the problem? I'll have a bath.

GARY: Just leave it out.

ADRIAN: You've lost me, Gary. They look clean, I'd say. Have 'em both. Ideal. Room service. Get a glass of beer thrown in and the sheets changed after. You'd better hurry. They'll be going.

GARY: Apart from anything else, they're not dogs, are they?

ADRIAN: What? What's this? They're not dogs? Are you saying they've got to be prostitutes? Oh, I see. No, that's all right because in these parts they don't make the distinction. I said: pay them enough you can piss on them.

GARY: Shut up!

ADRIAN: I would like you to explain to me the difference between you going out and finding a girl and offering her money to come back up here, and asking a girl who's already in the room, in fact already half in your bed?

GARY: You think you're being so clever, don't you?

The girls are ready to go out.

ADRIAN: Missed your chance. (*Fishes out a tip.*) Thank you. Thank you very much. (*They exit.*) Anyway, I'm going to have that bath. There was a time when I could have slept anywhere. Now I must have clean sheets.

Scene Three

A boat. We're at the destination of a boat trip to Ayuthya, the old capital city of Thailand. The boat is a very smart launch belonging to the Oriental Hotel. STEPHEN *would prefer to stay on it rather than set out on another expedition. It's hot and grey, and has briefly stopped raining.*

FRANCES: I don't want to walk around by myself.

STEPHEN: Nobody's going to jump on you.

FRANCES: I don't enjoy looking at things by myself. It's no fun. (*Pause.*) The rain's stopped.

STEPHEN: I'm quite happy to sit here.

FRANCES: There's no way of measuring anything unless you're with me. It's not the same. You look at something alone, it's different. It's not the same.

STEPHEN: Well I want to stay on the boat and you want me to come and look at more Buddhas. It's a quandary. What do we do?

FRANCES: Oh Stephen.

STEPHEN: Oh Stephen what?

FRANCES: You think banter is conversation, Stephen. Banter is instead of conversation.

STEPHEN: Well, as they say it takes two to banter.

FRANCES: I want this to be a real holiday. Something special. It doesn't happen any more. Us alone. Us alone properly, without Christopher, to spend time, to talk.

STEPHEN: It won't happen anyway. Once we get to Hong Kong I won't see you and Katie for dust.

FRANCES: We're not in Hong Kong.

STEPHEN: Hong Kong is my holiday, in case you'd forgotten . . . I'm working here.

FRANCES: Stephen, you have to, it's a gesture, you have to show your face at the factory, that's all. You know it.

EDWARD *comes rounding up stragglers.*

EDWARD: I think the guide's waiting for us.

FRANCES: Oh, right.

EDWARD: Seems like the rain's given up, anyway.

FRANCES: Yes.

STEPHEN: My wife and I are at loggerheads. She wants me to troop round this temple and I'm knackered.

FRANCES: Well.

STEPHEN: Not so much knackered as a bit fed up with all these bloody temples.

EDWARD: It's the Buddha's birthday.

FRANCES: I thought it was.

EDWARD: The guide's explaining. He's

very good, actually.

STEPHEN: I can't follow a word he's saying.

EDWARD: Yes, he's Dutch.

STEPHEN: Typical, isn't it? Get a Dutchman to be a guide for English tourists.

EDWARD: I expect he has to speak many languages besides English.

STEPHEN: That's his problem.

FRANCES: My husband thinks the whole world should speak English.

STEPHEN: No.

EDWARD: You're welcome to walk around with me if that would help.

FRANCES (*saying no*): Really.

EDWARD: I'm not an expert but I'm . . .

STEPHEN: You don't need to be. I could describe the inside of this temple without looking at it.

FRANCES: You have to exaggerate.

EDWARD: This one is the biggest. You can't see it all in one go. It's extraordinary. There's no point inside the building where you can get far enough away to see the whole thing.

STEPHEN: Ironic, isn't it, they spend all this money on worship – these temples . . . they'll do that and half the country's starving. You can tell the temple, it's the clean building made of stone not the corrugated rat huts, those warrens that look like miles of scrapyard. That's where the people live . . . the temples are white.

EDWARD: You can be angry about the poverty and still appreciate the culture. I am. I do.

STEPHEN: I'm not the slightest bit angry about it. You'll miss your guided tour.

FRANCES: Why have you never said that before? (*The polemic.*)

EDWARD: I'll . . . (*Exiting.*)

FRANCES: I will come with you if I may.

EDWARD: Right, but can we . . . (*Anxious to catch up.*)

STEPHEN: Wish Buddha happy birthday for me.

GARY *appears, looking for suitable surface to force off beer cap. He surveys the boat, river, the party exiting.*

GARY: Can't stand this weather.

STEPHEN: No.

GARY: I could do without living in my own sweat.

STEPHEN: Yes.

GARY: Why are they giving us a guided tour of the graveyards? My interest is strictly in the living bits.

STEPHEN: Have you had a walk round Patpong?

GARY: Oh yeah, done a recce in one of those motorbike things, but I've got a few addresses from a friend at home. A few special places.

STEPHEN: Right. What? Sort of . . . (*Prompting.*)

GARY: Like the man said, why go for something with a lot of miles on the clock?

STEPHEN: You mean in the sense of . . . (*Prompting.*)

GARY: You still can't be too careful. I'm a real boy scout, me. I've got enough antibiotics to paralyse a fucking elephant.

STEPHEN: Right. Otherwise . . . (*Prompting.*)

GARY: Otherwise, a touch of the early morning stings.

STEPHEN: Yes, I've noticed there's a lot of information about clinics.

GARY: Listen, if you were a germ in this country! Imagine, imagine being a germ in Bangkok.

STEPHEN: But it wouldn't stop you . . .? (*Prompting.*)

GARY: No, just got to make sure every-where you go's been nicely scrubbed.

STEPHEN: They say you can just do anything, get anything you want.

GARY: Oh yes.

STEPHEN: Some of the things you hear, people want, people will pay for makes you laugh, ridiculous things. I've heard people will pay a lot of money to lie under glass tables while women squat on the

tables and . . . as if they were on the loo.

GARY: Mental. No, I'm normal, me. Up against the wall I'm happy as a sand boy. (*A short laugh.*) Look at the state of that river. Swim in that!

STEPHEN: They do though, don't they?

GARY: It's like when you've washed up after cooking curry, the big pots, and it won't go down the plug 'cause it's too thick and greasy. Do you like curry?

STEPHEN: Yes. Oh yes. I like . . . not too . . .

GARY: I wouldn't eat them here though. Bugger that. We were eating last night and there was a lizard by my foot staring at me so I started looking and they're everywhere. They'll be straight in the pot a bit of sauce over the top and it's King Prawn Masala. I can't stand the way they move, lizards. That's one thing I've learned. Don't let them cover anything with sauce.

STEPHEN: And these special, these addresses, you'll go and, you'll check them out?

GARY: Oh yes.

STEPHEN: With your, is he a, what is he? Your colleague?

GARY: Well, we don't kiss.

STEPHEN: No.

GARY: Yeah, he'll come I expect. He makes out he's not interested. That's his view on it, but he'll come. He's my boss.

STEPHEN: What's the business?

GARY: Fashion.

STEPHEN: Right.

GARY: You probably bought your shirt from one of our shops.

STEPHEN: My wife kits me out.

GARY: I have to say you should tell her how old you are. Did you bring her with you or is that your secretary?

STEPHEN: My secretary's twenty-two, no, yes it's my wife, she's my wife, my secretary as it happens is exactly the kind of woman you'd want to bring with you. Not that she'd come. She does tai chi. She'd break my fingers if I . . . the fact of the matter is she got attacked, well practically. She was followed, chased, by a group of, a gang, and they, I don't think they actually but they frightened her. Quite badly. She has this way of not looking at you.

GARY: They can go frigid, can't they?

STEPHEN (*agreeing*): She's very nice, I'll tell you she's one of those women . . . I'll give you an example. Last week, before we left, she had a top on and it was slashed down one side, so depending on how she sat, if she was leaning a particular way you could see all her (*Demonstrates.*) just . . . and so all afternoon I kept, it was really distracting, and I'm just supposed to, and then she's just as likely as not to turn round and tell me to (*Short sigh.*) . . .

GARY: What's her name?

STEPHEN: Uh . . . Maggie.

GARY: Well, if Maggie comes on like that but is not prepared to take the consequences, what I'm saying is if she won't go down on you she's a cunt. Half of London have got this attitude about behaviour. It's a disgrace.

STEPHEN: Anyway, it's my wife who's here.

GARY: Who's buggered off with our dentist friend.

STEPHEN: I can't face another temple.

GARY: Questions have to be asked about old Steradent features. You don't mind her going off with him?

STEPHEN: I doubt if they'll get into heavy petting in the temple.

GARY: A fuck begins with a look in my experience.

STEPHEN: You can't stop people looking at each other. I can't stop her looking at people.

GARY: He's got bad breath. That's a joke, isn't it. Unforgivable in his profession. Extremely lacking in class.

STEPHEN: These addresses? Are they clubs or what?

GARY: What? Yes. Clubs. Clubs and private addresses. So you want to come along then, is that it?

STEPHEN: No, I . . .

GARY: I suppose the problem is giving your wife the slip?

STEPHEN: Well I wouldn't go as far . . .

GARY: Or does she get off on . . .?

STEPHEN: No. No. I suppose if I were by myself . . . no but my wife's not . . .

EDWARD *returns*.

GARY: What have you done with his Mrs?

EDWARD: She's making her way back.

GARY: Chivalrous.

EDWARD: Your friend is walking with her.

GARY: Is he? (*Gives* STEPHEN *a conspiratorial look.*)

EDWARD (*to* STEPHEN): It's your loss, you know, sitting here. It's a marvellous temple.

GARY: We'll take your word for it.

EDWARD (*slyly*): There were dancing girls.

GARY: What? A disco?

EDWARD: I went to dental school with a chap just like you.

GARY: Terrific.

EDWARD: He liked to inject himself with valium.

GARY: Terrific.

EDWARD (*to* STEPHEN): Your wife says I can buy special computers for dentists.

STEPHEN: Yes, software packages – records and accounts packages. Yes.

EDWARD: I don't know anything about computers.

GARY: I thought he was going to say he didn't know anything about teeth.

EDWARD: I do know they make a lot of computer components in Asia.

STEPHEN: That's right. We've got a factory here.

EDWARD: Your company?

STEPHEN: Yes.

EDWARD: I read somewhere companies farm out work to places like Bangkok which workers in Europe and America won't do.

STEPHEN: What do you mean?

EDWARD: Work that wouldn't pass the scrutiny of Health and Safety at Work legislation.

STEPHEN: I have to say that's actually a fiction.

EDWARD: Possibly. I read that the eye gets damaged doing repetitive . . . is it welding work? . . . on to the circuit boards. No, they're not called circuit boards, the . . .

STEPHEN: I know what you mean.

EDWARD: And I'm wrong.

STEPHEN: We do ship work out. It's a multinational. There's a global labour force. Different skills in different places.

EDWARD: I thought it was just that in the East the labour was cheap and uncomplaining.

GARY (stirring): Heavy!

STEPHEN: I'm not responsible for the policy for . . .

EDWARD: I wasn't suggesting you were.

GARY (stirring): I think he was.

EDWARD: It was an article I read.

STEPHEN: As it happens, Asian women are particularly good at bonding chips. They use gold wire. The chips are minute. It's a very delicate operation. The women have tiny hands and they're patient.

EDWARD: That's all right then.

STEPHEN: As I said it's not my policy.

EDWARD: I'll have to find out more about these dentist packs.

STEPHEN (irritable): Did you say Fran was coming back or what?

GARY (to STEPHEN): He's winding you up.

EDWARD (heated): I'm not talking about Stephen, I'm talking about multinationals. (Checks.) Stephen?

STEPHEN: I happen to have a certain loyalty.

EDWARD: No, but I'm saying you're not responsible for what, that's what you said yourself.

STEPHEN: You see, people want the most

up to date technology at the most competitive prices but they don't want to know how it's achieved.

EDWARD: What?

STEPHEN: Your Dental Records Program would use semi-conductors bonded in Bangkok is what I'm saying.

EDWARD: Well then I don't suppose . . .

STEPHEN: Everyone is so pious.

EDWARD: You think it's all right, then do you, that we abuse – we abuse, OK? – so many people, peoples, countries, so that we can . . .

STEPHEN: You're distorting, you're absolutely distorting.

EDWARD (simultaneously): . . . enjoy certain creature comforts because I don't . . .

GARY (glee): Aye-Aye!

STEPHEN: And there is no reliable evidence about eye deterioration.

EDWARD: This was a medical journal!

STEPHEN: If you want to talk about boredom then I'd agree with you it's a pretty boring job.

EDWARD: I bet it is!

STEPHEN: That's what I'm saying, it's bloody boring!

EDWARD: And menial and appallingly paid!

STEPHEN: Yes! OK!

EDWARD: – you know – and I've been to these hostels, actually, where they accommodate these women and you wouldn't live in them!

STEPHEN: OK, so let's hear the solution!

EDWARD: Ach!

STEPHEN: Because they're starving in the north, they're starving in the south. They kiss us, they literally kiss us for the work, they burn incense, they dance because we give them a job so don't!

EDWARD: What did your company, what were your company profits –

STEPHEN: Christ!

GARY (to STEPHEN): Ask him what he makes.

EDWARD: I'll tell you how much I make.

STEPHEN: OK.

EDWARD: I don't believe this.

FRANCES *and* ADRIAN *return.*

FRANCES: Stephen, you missed a wonderful show, wonderful dancers, has Edward told you? And an exquisite temple, honestly, the most beautiful: sod's law.

GARY: Edward's been winding your husband up something rotten.

FRANCES: What?

GARY: We've been highly political on the old boat front.

FRANCES: What's going on?

STEPHEN: Nothing.

EDWARD: Nothing.

FRANCES: Stephen?

STEPHEN: Nothing.

EDWARD (*to* STEPHEN): I'm sorry. It's a hobby horse.

STEPHEN: Yes. (*To* FRANCES:) You forgot your camera.

FRANCES: Did I?

STEPHEN: Obviously engrossed.

FRANCES (*to* ADRIAN): We were, weren't we? (*To* STEPHEN:) I was. Adrian was telling me – you've met Adrian haven't you?

ADRIAN: We talked at the airport and in the lobby.

STEPHEN: Right.

FRANCES: Adrian was telling me that – have you seen that next to houses, in the gardens, there are like elaborate birds' houses, like little temples . . . ?

EDWARD: Spirit houses – they're spirit houses.

FRANCES: Yes, that's right.

EDWARD: Yes, the thing is, Thai people, Buddhists, believe there's a spirit living on every plot of ground . . . so obviously if they build on it, they're building on top of a spirit's house, so what they do is to build another little house, tiny, in which the spirit can live and they even put food . . . and (*he trails off as he realises he's stolen*

FRAN's *thunder.*) I'm sorry, was that what you were going to . . .?

FRANCES: I think I'll see if I can get a drink or something.

EDWARD: It was, wasn't it?

ADRIAN: I'll have a look.

STEPHEN: No I'll, what do you want?

EDWARD: I'll do it.

STEPHEN: No.

FRANCES: Really, it's –

EDWARD: I'd like to. Please. I would like to . . .

FRANCES: All right.

EDWARD: What would everyone like?

A WAITER *appears. Permanent smile. Polite. Frosty.*

WAITER: I'm to tell you that we are serving buffet dinner in the Captain's Mess.

STEPHEN: Can we get a drink?

WAITER: We are serving drinks in Captain's Mess.

EDWARD: I can go along, ahead. Save places in the queue.

WAITER: No queue.

EDWARD: Good. Can we order wine?

WAITER: Anything you like.

EDWARD: Chilled wine?

WAITER: Anything you like.

EDWARD: I'll get a bottle of chilled wine, shall I?

They're exiting: STEPHEN, FRANCES *and* EDWARD.

GARY: Questions have to be asked about old dental floss.

ADRIAN *doesn't respond. He's settling down for a gaze at the water.*

GARY: Nice walk?

ADRIAN: What?

GARY: He's desperate, the husband, Stephen . . .

ADRIAN: Is he?

GARY: It's so funny, because he adopts this kind of pose, of curiosity: what do

you think about the weather? about
Bangkok? about Buddha? and he's really
asking you if you've managed it yet, and if
so how, where, how much and is there
any way he could join you.

ADRIAN (*weary of* GARY): Do you know
where we are?

GARY: On a boat.

ADRIAN: How old are you?

GARY: What?

ADRIAN: Have you got any idea of the
name of this place? Do you think we're to
the north of Bangkok? The south? Could
you point to Bangkok on the map?

GARY: No, we had a choice at school
between geography and sex. But listen, I
hear it was a really interesting temple?

ADRIAN: Just for the record, because it's a
pity, and because I'm not going to allow
you the pleasure, it used to be – this place
– it was supposed to be the most beautiful
city in the East at one time, and now it's
just rubble and these broken bits of stone,
but it's a wonder, it's something to see
and you sit on your arse and . . . there
are people who have walked for miles,
who are sodden, carrying little baskets of,
I don't know, bits of food and flowers and
gifts to give to these stones and they're
throwing counters and burning incense
and . . . whole families and dancers, and
you're sat here nursing your hard-on.

GARY: Everyone's very keen on these
dancers.

ADRIAN: That's right.

GARY (*goading*): And how was Mrs
Stephen? Was she interesting?

ADRIAN: Go away, Gary.

GARY: I tell you what impressed me: those
fish, the carp this morning, completely
brilliant. In the pond, wherever it was,
this morning, eating rolls, bigger than
their mouths, bigger than their stomachs,
huge fuckers eating everything, like
submarines, and you watch the people
with their, with these rolls, 'cause they're
not throwing for the little sprats, nice
colours, lovely, no, they're chucking for
the big bastards, cruising along with their
jaws open, ugly, perfect. That impressed
me.

ADRIAN: And what do you deduce from
this observation, Gary?

GARY: Oh, bastards win.

FRANCES *appears.*

FRANCES: I wasn't sure whether you'd
realised they've started serving, looks
very good, good fish . . .

GARY: I'm coming.

FRANCES: Adrian was telling me that you
are his best salesman.

GARY: He's a sweetie, that Adrian. I had a
nice chat with your hubbie. I'll see you
chaps down below.

FRANCES: Yes, I'm following on.

Exit GARY.

FRANCES: Are you coming down,
Adrian?

ADRIAN: It's too hot to eat.

FRANCES: Yes.

*A pause. They stare out at the river. All
this brief exchange is charged with mutual
attraction.*

ADRIAN: What are those kids selling?

FRANCES: Salt, I think. I enjoyed our
walk. Thank you.

ADRIAN: So did I.

FRANCES: What next, do you know?

ADRIAN: I think we go back.

FRANCES: Stephen hates these things,
tours, organised things. I rather enjoy
them. I like guides and . . .

ADRIAN: Right.

FRANCES: I didn't actually mean that,
anyway. I mean what next in the sense of
us sightseeing together, or, you know,
when you said . . . on the walk . . .

ADRIAN: Yes, I'd like that.

FRANCES: Yes. (STEPHEN *appears.*) I
was just coming.

STEPHEN: If I'd known you were coming
up here I would have sent your fish back.

FRANCES: It's OK.

STEPHEN (*to* ADRIAN): Not hungry?

ADRIAN: No.

They exit. ADRIAN *sits.*

Scene Four

A clothing factory.
A lobby. A sort of reception area where reception space is at a premium, like a parish priest's vestibule. A small room with a table and two or three chairs and some bizarre furnishings.

OWNER: Can I offer you gentlemen a refreshment?

GARY: You can offer me one. I'd like a beer.

OWNER: Singha? Carlsberg Special?

GARY: The coldest.

OWNER: And for you, Mister West?

ADRIAN: Can I drink with you?

OWNER: I drink tea. I'm afraid.

ADRIAN: Tea would be good.

OWNER: Excuse me for a moment or two.

The OWNER *exits. A beat.*

GARY: He speaks English better than me.

ADRIAN: And he's got better manners.

GARY: That's easy. What is this place? His garage?

ADRIAN: This is it. He probably makes everything here.

GARY: Himself?

ADRIAN: I wouldn't like to guess how many girls he's got working here.

GARY: Will he show us?

ADRIAN: No. They won't show you anything other than the garment. It's the same in Hong Kong. No questions about how, just about how much, how many.

GARY: Are you seriously thinking you might buy from him?

ADRIAN: Depends how much, how many.

GARY: There's no point in buying denim.

ADRIAN: He'll make anything.

GARY: I'm just saying, we can't give denim away. Frank rang up, was offering me a lorry load, any name, two pound a pair.

ADRIAN: Just remember it's not barrow boy tactics out here. We look and we stay quiet. Everything is done quietly. If you're good I might take you out tonight.

GARY: Mum, I'm on a promise.

ADRIAN: Three days' celibacy I thought would be too much for you.

GARY: But on the third day it rose again.

GARY is distracted by his stomach.

I knew I'd get the runs.

ADRIAN: You should be more careful.

GARY: There's a disco going on in here. (*His stomach.*) Bastard. That was that buffet yesterday. That's why you're all right.

OWNER (*returning*): One very cold beer. And for us, Mr West. (*The tea.*)

GARY: Ta.

ADRIAN: Thank you.

OWNER: How do you like Bangkok?

GARY: Yeah. OK.

ADRIAN: We spent yesterday on the river.

OWNER: To Ayuthya.

ADRIAN: That's right.

OWNER: A good day to go, the Buddha's birthday.

ADRIAN: Yeah.

OWNER: But the weather.

ADRIAN: Not great.

OWNER: My wife and I call this weather American weather.

ADRIAN: Oh?

OWNER: I don't know why. The Americans are not – in this part of the world – some people say they have had a bad influence on us . . . too much Coca Cola, other things we copy . . . For myself, I have many American friends but we still call this bad weather American weather. Just an expression.

ADRIAN: Well it's very American weather.

OWNER: Will you stay and eat with me?

ADRIAN: Thank you, no.

GARY: Anyway, I've got gutrot.

OWNER: I'm so sorry. I am afraid this is very common. Same for me when I visited London. I have upset stomach for many days. If you want the lavatory . . .

GARY: I'll let you know.

OWNER: So, the weather American, the stomach unhappy, anything good?

GARY: Cold beer.

OWNER: Good. (*A gear change.*) So.

ADRIAN: So.

OWNER: How can I be of service?

ADRIAN: I don't know.

OWNER: I understand you may be interested in buying from my factory.

ADRIAN: Then you misunderstand. I have a very good relationship with my supplier in Hong Kong.

OWNER: Quite so. But perhaps, for interest's sake, you would like to see some examples of our work. I think you will agree it is of the highest quality.

ADRIAN: Unfortunately, in London certain people speak badly of Bangkok. They say expect poor delivery, perhaps not top quality finishing, uneven dye, I don't know . . .

OWNER: And yet: here you are. More tea?

ADRIAN: Thank you. There are big changes in Hong Kong.

OWNER: Oh yes. 1997.

ADRIAN: Yes, 1997 but also more and more legislation, union difficulties . . .

OWNER: I understand. Too much light. Times change. Big light on Hong Kong. In Bangkok, still many shadows, lots of shadows.

ADRIAN: That's right.

OWNER: I understand.

He claps his hands.

I have arranged a small entertainment. This is Minna and Malee.

Two attractive girls appear, one wearing a skirt and a blouse, the other wearing a dress . . . both smart. MINNA carries a large cassette recorder and MALEE some clothes – another dress, a pair of jeans and a tee shirt.

GARY: Hello.

The girls smile.

OWNER: This is a small demonstration. A few minutes.

He nods at MINNA who turns on the cassette which plays middle of the road, slightly dated, disco music. She starts to dance, then MALEE dances too, just jogging around.

Everything the girls wear was made by us, all 100 per cent cotton, machine washable.

The girls turn round.

GARY: Very nice.

OWNER: Thank you. These designs are our own. We will also make up to any pattern. You must, of course, examine the workmanship.

He nods again. The girls undress, still attempting to move gracefully. Not a striptease. They wear bikinis.

The bikinis is also made by us.

The girls give GARY and ADRIAN their clothes. The girls redress in the second outfits: jeans and blouse, and a dress.

GARY: I had a feeling they were going to do that.

The girls dance.

I think we might have to examine the finish on these as well.

He laughs, he's quite nervous, excited; the girls smile.

ADRIAN: Shall we talk about money?

OWNER: I don't want to talk about money.

GARY: Well, we talked about the weather: it's lousy.

OWNER (*to ADRIAN*): I think perhaps your friend would prefer to be entertained a little more . . .

GARY: Do they work for you?

OWNER: Yes. They have been with me for a long time. See how happy they are. They don't sew any more, of course.

GARY: Oh?

OWNER: Three or four years: time to do new job, the hands become . . . the fingers are tired, not so good.

ADRIAN: So then what?

OWNER: These girls are very pretty. I like to show my clothes being worn . . . on a body.

ADRIAN: Until the bodies get tired.

OWNER: Oh, sometimes my wife says she thinks I run a hotel, not a workshop. Would you like to look at the jeans? Very good.

GARY: Yeah.

ADRIAN: We're not interested in denim.

OWNER: See! No harm in seeing. These are Italian designs.

He nods to the girl in jeans. She removes them.

ADRIAN: Are you leaving these girls with us?

OWNER: I had thought you might like their company.

ADRIAN: So as we don't confuse business and pleasure.

OWNER: Absolutely.

ADRIAN: We're very happy about the girls, thank you.

OWNER: Just so.

ADRIAN: Gary? Are you happy with the girls?

GARY: Yeah thanks. Very happy.

ADRIAN: The clothes, of course, are a different matter.

OWNER: Quite.

ADRIAN: So let's keep the clothes. Perhaps the best thing would be to send the girls away, then, just until we've finished our business together.

The girls remove all the clothes.

Thank you.

GARY: See you later.

One girl picks up the tape recorder, smiling, goes to hand it to ADRIAN.

OWNER: From my company with our compliments.

The girl turns off the cassette machine and in the process drops it. It stops playing. Nobody speaks.

Butter fingers.

Scene Five

The bedroom. STEPHEN, FRANCES.
    FRANCES *is in the room,* STEPHEN *in the bathroom. As the scene begins, we listen, with* FRANCES, *to the unmistakable noises of lovemaking coming through the wall from the adjacent bedroom.* FRANCES *turns up the air-conditioning. Then* STEPHEN *enters, sporting a new Lacoste tee shirt.*

FRANCES: Not bad for two pounds fifty.

STEPHEN: It's all right, isn't it?

FRANCES: It's marvellous.

STEPHEN: I think it actually is a Lacoste.

FRANCES: I think so.

STEPHEN: No really.

FRANCES: We should ask Adrian or Gary. They'll know, of course.

STEPHEN: Not necessarily. It's not stuck on, it's sewn. (*Pulling at the label.*) How much was it?

FRANCES: Before we beat her down? Well, 140 baht, so that's four, practically five . . .

STEPHEN: Even that's a fraction of what, I've seen them for over twenty-five at home.

FRANCES: Well, I'm very pleased with myself.

STEPHEN: I must say I was impressed, a new side of you, pretty ferocious.

FRANCES (*prodding him*): Stomach.

STEPHEN: Ach.

FRANCES: You can't wear a Lacoste tee shirt and bulge over the top of your belt.

STEPHEN: Stodgy food.

FRANCES: Hmm. What shall I wear?

STEPHEN: I must go the the gym. There's no time. It's impossible. I paid all that bloody money and I never go. I save a couple of quid on a tee shirt and . . . I don't even get a lunch break these days.

FRANCES: Let's go somewhere nice tonight, eh? There's that list Katie gave us.

STEPHEN: We can't go mad.

FRANCES: They're not all expensive, I don't think, they're not, I'm sure.

(*Scrabbling around*) . . . We could take a tuk-tuk and hold hands.

STEPHEN: OK.

FRANCES (*happy*): Can we?

STEPHEN: Yeah.

FRANCES: It's all right, isn't it? Being together . . .

STEPHEN: We could even go on to a club or something after.

FRANCES (*finding this ominous*): Right.

She takes off her kimono and hunts around for something to wear. She's in her underwear.

I'd love to buy a silk dress while we're here. Or Hong Kong. Thai silk would be nice. What do you think? (*She touches him.*) Darling? (*No response.*) Stephen?

STEPHEN: Can you hear anything?

FRANCES: Hear what?

STEPHEN: Hang on. (*He turns off the air-conditioner.*) Listen . . . (*They listen together.*) That's from thing's room, your friend, Adrian.

FRANCES: Is it? It's a twin room. They're sharing.

STEPHEN: No, listen . . .

She starts pulling on some clothes.

(*Frisson.*) Bloody hell.

FRANCES: Bloody hell what?

STEPHEN: Well there's obviously something going on.

FRANCES: Stephen.

STEPHEN: What?

FRANCES: Are you just going to sit there and listen?

STEPHEN: Do you think they're both, I mean, how many people can you hear? Bloody hell.

FRANCES: Well, are you?

STEPHEN: I tell you one thing which is very interesting – for all the bragging this is the first time, because these walls are pretty thin, evidently, and this is the first time I've heard anything. Do you think they'd both, with the other in the room, I can't imagine.

FRANCES: Clearly you can imagine.

STEPHEN: It's early evening.

FRANCES: And?

STEPHEN: Well, it's just early.

FRANCES: You mean it's not dark.

STEPHEN: You know exactly what I mean.

FRANCES: Funny, isn't it? Because – it's exciting you, isn't it? You're with me in a bedroom and I'm half naked and we could make love, we don't have our son barging in, or your work, we could just make love here, now, in the early evening . . . and you're getting turned on by the sounds in the next room.

STEPHEN: Do you want to make love?

There's a long pause. STEPHEN *can't help listening.*

FRANCES: I don't miss Christopher, you know.

STEPHEN: What do you mean?

FRANCES: I don't miss him. I hope he's all right . . . but I don't miss him.

STEPHEN: OK.

FRANCES: I just want you to know that.

STEPHEN: Well OK you've told me.

FRANCES: Sometimes I don't like him very much, Stephen.

STEPHEN: He can be naughty, he's a boy, he's seven, he's not . . .

FRANCES: No, I mean, I'm saying I don't like his personality, not that he's a child, or a responsibility . . . I don't like him.

STEPHEN: That's the point, the responsibility, you don't actually mean you don't like your own son. It's just the, obviously every single day to have to, obviously it's going to, it's not Christopher and it's not you, I'd probably . . .

FRANCES: Right.

STEPHEN: Well, isn't that right?

FRANCES: That's probably it then.

STEPHEN: We should send him a postcard.

FRANCES: I did.

STEPHEN *can't help listening.*

STEPHEN: Remind me later to buy one.

FRANCES: Stephen, are you listening to me?

STEPHEN: You said that it, you agreed with me about what I said about Christopher. Christ.

FRANCES: Do you wish you were in there with them?

STEPHEN: No. (*Pause.*) No.

FRANCES: I'm not criticising you.

STEPHEN: Aren't you?

FRANCES: I think, in other circumstances, I could find it erotic, listening.

STEPHEN (*not believing*): Sure.

FRANCES: Why do you hit me sometimes when we're in bed?

STEPHEN: What do you mean, hit you?

FRANCES: When we make love. You've hit me.

STEPHEN (*appalled*): Don't be, I haven't, don't be ridiculous.

FRANCES: You have, Stephen.

STEPHEN: I've slapped, this is ridiculous, not even slapped, that's the wrong word, I've in the most playful sense, I would never hit you and you should say if you didn't like, I obviously, I assumed you quite, otherwise you would have said, we're talking about years, Frances, Christ. I would never hit you.

FRANCES: Now I've said then.

STEPHEN: That makes me feel terrible. Terrible.

FRANCES: You're right, I should have said.

STEPHEN: You should have done. Bloody hell. Fucking hell.

FRANCES: I don't want to stay in this room any longer now. Let's go out.

STEPHEN: Sometimes when I think about you it's like a bathroom and it's white and tiled and locked.

FRANCES: What is?

STEPHEN: What is what?

FRANCES: What is like a bathroom and

locked and white?

STEPHEN: You. I just said. Just sometimes when I think I suppose I don't know what you're thinking. Because you can be very cold.

FRANCES: What are you going to do Stephen? Because you can lie there and eavesdrop all evening, that's all right with me, if that's what you want, but I'm, I would like to eat something.

STEPHEN: I'm waiting for you, I'm ready.

Scene Six

EDWARD, *alone in his hotel room, wishing he were elsewhere.*
A knock. EDWARD *answers the door.*

EDWARD: Yes?

NET: Mr Net.

EDWARD: Hang on.

EDWARD *inspects his room then takes door off latch and lets* NET *in.*

NET: Good evening.

EDWARD: Now then.

NET: Happy room?

EDWARD: Very happy.

NET: Everything work?

EDWARD: Everything works.

NET: Air-conditioning? (*Checking.*)

EDWARD: Fine. (*Points at it, whining away.*)

NET: Net tooth . . . very good. No problem. Very great.

EDWARD: Oh good.

NET: Weather not good not bad. Half-half.

EDWARD: That's it.

NET: These months always.

EDWARD: It's OK. I went on a good boat trip yesterday. Very interesting.

NET: How much you pay? Ayuthya or Floating Market?

EDWARD: Ayuthya.

NET: How much you pay?

EDWARD: Three hundred baht.

NET: Three hundred baht!

EDWARD: Fixed price.

NET: Next time, speak to Net. Two hundred baht, no problem.

EDWARD: Two hundred?

NET: No problem.

EDWARD: Well.

NET: So, tonight you like nice girl?

EDWARD: No.

NET: Maybe Edward find wife in Bangkok? That case Net introduce Edward to sister or cousin not bumsin girl.

EDWARD: I'm not ungrateful just not interested.

NET: Understand.

EDWARD: So no point in asking. OK?

NET: OK. No problem. Just want my friend to know very special price.

EDWARD: I'm sure it would be very special.

NET: Talking maybe half price.

EDWARD: Thank you.

NET: Net have present for Edward. For toothbrush. This is present. Cassette. Music. Net favourite song. (*Produces cassette.*)

EDWARD: For me? That's really kind, Net. Thank you. Are you sure?

NET: Listen now?

EDWARD: I can't. I don't have a machine.

NET: No problem. Net have machine in Hotel Minibus. Edward come with Net to listen.

EDWARD: Oh no, I'll, it can be a surprise when I get to Hong Kong, eh? Don't . . .

NET: What you do this evening?

EDWARD: Read.

NET: Read?

EDWARD: Yes.

NET: All evening?

EDWARD: I expect so. Maybe a walk. I don't know. Probably just read.

NET: What you want to do?

EDWARD: I enjoy reading. Please Net don't ask me to any more things. I don't like, much, to do things. Read about them, but not to do.

NET: Net understand. Watch sex show maybe. Net know good place.

EDWARD: No. What do you mean, sex show?

NET: Boy and girl. Whole thing. Just watch. No problem.

EDWARD: I don't think so. To tell you the truth I'm quite curious . . . I'm quite interested in just seeing these places, just driving along the roads . . . Patpong . . .

NET: Patpong: yes: OK.

EDWARD: No I'm just saying, I'm – not to go in anywhere or stop or speak to anyone – but to look, out of curiosity.

NET: Just look. Net understand. Maybe stop if Edward wants. Not want, not stop. OK. Net wait downstairs. Edward come down five minutes. Net drive Edward Patpong. No problem.

EDWARD (*flustered*): Ten minutes. Fifteen minutes. Fifteen minutes.

NET: OK.

EDWARD: Just to drive around, play your cassette.

NET: All no problem. Net take care friend.

EDWARD: And your wife doesn't mind, she's not expecting you home?

NET: No, because wife understand Net maybe – tonight no charge for friend – but maybe friend do favour or give Net small tip, but wife understand everything anyway. Good Buddhist.

EDWARD: No . . . Well obviously I'll buy you something to eat. We'll eat together, yes? And I must pay you for petrol and, anyway, anyway: why Good Buddhist? Why do you say that about your wife?

NET: Don't know. (*Shrugs.*) Suppose . . . (*Considers.*) Don't know but she always follow teaching, wife must be good wife. Just do what Net say.

EDWARD: Is that what she's taught?

NET (*shrugs*): Guess so. Net not very religious. Love Buddha. Try do what right and wrong. You follow?

EDWARD: I think so.

NET: Some day sun, some day rain. Life is weather. No problem.

EDWARD: That's right.

NET: OK. Net see you downstairs in ten minutes.

But EDWARD *has, of course, completely thawed.*

EDWARD: Net, just, listen: you might as well wait. I won't be a minute.

Scene Seven

Much later that evening. The coffee shop. A foursome in progress. ADRIAN *and* GARY *are drunkish,* MINNA *and* MALEE *are worse for wear, but not drunk, not animated. Weary hostesses who have been fed at last.*
On the table, full ashtrays, empty singha bottles, liqueur glasses, cans of coke: the evening's debris.

GARY: What's the score about later then?

ADRIAN: I don't know.

GARY: Same bedroom?

ADRIAN: I'm not intending to sleep with anybody. Are you?

GARY: Well . . .

ADRIAN: What for?

GARY: What do you mean what for?

ADRIAN: How many ways are there?

GARY: You haven't even had yours yet. She's fallen asleep. Look at that!

ADRIAN *shakes* MINNA *(his companion) who's dropped off.*

ADRIAN: Eh!

She wakes up, startled. Eats a bit.

GARY: She's got bored waiting. Don't you fancy her?

ADRIAN: Not a lot.

GARY: I wouldn't mind it. What about a swap?

ADRIAN: No.

GARY: Why not?

ADRIAN: Because I've formed a

relationship with Minna, haven't I? (*He shakes her.*) Eh? You can't just throw that out of the window.

GARY: You're a bastard. You're winding me up.

ADRIAN: Besides I want to get some sleep and if you swap you'll be . . . I don't want to have to listen to you.

GARY: You might learn something.

ADRIAN (*somewhere else*): You reckon?

GARY: Well, what about giving me another half hour . . . If I go up ahead now . . . I'll go up with her for half an hour, eh?

ADRIAN: It'll drop off.

GARY: Oh no, it's very solid. Look she's gone again, she's completely . . . she's in a trance.

ADRIAN: She's knackered.

GARY: Malee's all right though, isn't she? Look: first division. (*He prods her affectionately. She smiles. He looks over to* MINNA.) Go on, let's swap and I'll just have half an hour's worth. (*Smiles at* MINNA, *who smiles, tired, back.*)

ADRIAN: They're both ready to go home.

GARY: I don't think so. I bet they're having a bloody good evening in comparison.

ADRIAN: In comparison to what?

GARY: Come on: we haven't hurt them, and we've fed them. I bet this is a great evening for them. I'm not joking. Look in her bag.

ADRIAN: What?

GARY: Look in her bag – Oy, wake up! Oy gorgeous! Wake up! (*He shakes her.*) She's really struggling, isn't she? Just open your bag, let us see. We won't take anything. (*To* MALEE:) Tell her we won't take anything. I just want to see inside. (*Puts out his hands.*) Your bag. (*He takes it, opens it up . . . Folded inside a serviette is a piece of chicken and there's a small plastic bag filled with rice.*) Look at this: half the meal in this bag. Poor cow is probably starving. That's why she's nodding off: not used to eating so much.

ADRIAN: Give her the bag back.

GARY: I'm positive about this. Look at

that club tonight. Having to fondle those old guys – those old guys – they were German – with shorts on and those turkey legs, having to stroke bald heads and turkey legs. This is Christmas in comparison. Malee here agrees. (*Smiles.* MALEE *smiles. They hug, quite friendly.*)

ADRIAN: It's all one, I expect. If you have to do it. I expect it's all one. It's like a car park this place, isn't it?

GARY: Oh Christ, don't go mardi.

ADRIAN: I think they sent over their architects to train in London or Switzerland or somewhere and they went to the wrong place. They went to car park and garage design classes and they all came home and designed Bangkok and they think they've built a city but in fact they've built a car park.

GARY (*exploring* MALEE): Have you seen their fingers? They're all twisted, supposed to have pretty hands but they're ugly. It's like arthritis, like old people's hands.

MALEE *attempts to hide her fingers.*

ADRIAN: It probably is arthritis. You heard what their boss was saying: a few years sewing nonstop and their fingers are ruined.

GARY: Shall I go on up? I tell you what got me, about earlier, the first show, the sex show, no, was how afterwards, they were all bashful – did you see? With him covering himself. I thought that was really funny. After all that. I thought that was a real crease up.

ADRIAN: The thing is (*of* MINNA) I expect she's hoping she won't have to. If she just keeps her eyes closed then she'll fall asleep and wake up and she won't have had to.

GARY: You do fancy her don't you?

ADRIAN: Yeah. I expect so.

GARY: You do!

ADRIAN: Yeah. I do.

GARY: Well, you go on up, Adrian, go on, and we'll wait. Go on, and we'll have another drink. Yeah!

ADRIAN: I don't know. Maybe.

We join EDWARD *and* NET *who have just arrived after a happy tour and meal and chat.*

EDWARD: This time you must let me buy the drinks.

NET: No. My pleasure.

EDWARD: No, really, let me, you've spoiled me all evening.

NET: I am a man with a happy mouth: must celebrate. (*His teeth are OK.*)

EDWARD (*dismissive*): Oh . . .

NET: Half lager?

EDWARD: Half lager, chai. (*Yes.*)

NET: Chai! Chai!

EDWARD: Chai kawpkun. (*Yes thank you.*)

NET: Kawpkun! (*He slaps* EDWARD's *back then goes off to get lagers.*) Chai kawpkun!

EDWARD *alone, has to acknowledge the foursome. He nods.*

GARY: All right?

EDWARD: Now then. (*In gruff Barnsley greeting.*)

GARY: Good night?

EDWARD: Yes, thanks.

GARY: What you get up to?

EDWARD: Oh, had a drive round.

GARY: I bet you did. (*To* ADRIAN:) He had a drive round. (*To* EDWARD:) So did we. Took a few snaps and all, eh? (EDWARD *has his camera with him.*)

EDWARD: I did as it happens.

GARY: They'll never see the chemists, eh? Eh? (*To* ADRIAN:) He'll be developing them at home. (*To* EDWARD:) Oy, come on, come and join us.

EDWARD: I'm being bought a drink.

GARY: That's all right, bring your friend (*Loaded.*) and pull up a chair. Come on.

EDWARD: Really . . .

NET *returns with the lagers.* GARY *addresses him:*

GARY: Oy . . . You're being invited to come and join us.

NET: Oh. Thank you.

GARY: That's all right. Come on then. Come and join me. Adrian's just off upstairs. He's got to have a chat with Minna, his friend.

EDWARD: We don't want to disturb . . .

GARY: No, a private chat upstairs. (*To NET who's come across:*) I'm Gary, this is Minna and Malee and here's Adrian.

NET: I am Net.

EDWARD *reluctantly comes over. To ADRIAN:*

EDWARD: Don't let us keep you.

NET: You meet nice Thai girls?

GARY: Yeah.

NET: Have good evening?

GARY: Oh yeah brilliant.

NET: Us too. Very good evening, much laughing.

GARY: Oh yeah, we laughed and all. Lot of chatting, lot of laughing.

NET: Edward make Net's teeth very happy. Great friends.

GARY: Oh yeah?

EDWARD: Net's insisted on taking me out to show his gratitude. I didn't even do anything. Gave him some oil of cloves and a toothbrush. I didn't catch your friends' names . . .

GARY: Minna and Malee.

EDWARD: Hello.

MALEE *smiles.* MINNA*'s too tired.*

GARY: They're presents.

EDWARD: What's that?

GARY: The women. They're presents. On loan.

EDWARD: It wouldn't surprise me.

NET: Now Net tell Edward his special present.

EDWARD: Yes?

NET: Same present as your friend. Tonight Net arrange pretty girl come to your room.

GARY: Whooo!

EDWARD (*nervous laugh*): What?

NET: No charge. Net arrange. Nicer girl than these. Really. Very nice, very young, very clean, honest to God. All arranged. Surprise.

GARY: Who's a jammy bastard?

NET: Edward, Net's special friend.

STEPHEN *and* FRANCES *enter arm in arm. They've also had a good evening. They've come for a nightcap.* FRANCES *tries to steer* STEPHEN *straight out again.*

STEPHEN (*to* FRANCES, *nonplussed*): What?

ADRIAN: Hello.

STEPHEN: Evening.

FRANCES: Hello.

ADRIAN: You should join us. We're having an impromptu party. Come on, I'll get the chairs . . .

GARY (*to* ADRIAN): You've woken up.

FRANCES: I'm tired actually.

STEPHEN: Well . . .

GARY: We're all going to bed in a minute.

STEPHEN: Fine. Darling?

FRANCES: I said: I'm tired.

ADRIAN *returns with a chair and a waitress who carries the second chair and then hovers for the drinks order.*

ADRIAN: What are you drinking?

FRANCES: I think we're going up to bed.

ADRIAN: Oh.

STEPHEN *is fascinated by the women.*

STEPHEN: Come on, let's have a quick one. Yes? (FRANCES *impassive. To* ADRIAN:) Whisky please.

FRANCES: Lemon tea.

STEPHEN: Have a drink.

ADRIAN: One whisky, one lemon tea. Anyone else? (*To the women:*) Cokes? (*No takers.*) No? (*To* GARY:) You?

GARY: Southern Comfort. Ta.

Waitress exits, ADRIAN *gets up again.*

Now where you going?

ADRIAN (*exiting*): Guess.

GARY: So, this is Minna, Malee.

EDWARD: And this is Net. And this is Frances and Stephen.

NET: We met already. Net have to fix air-conditioning in your room.

STEPHEN: That's right. Yes. It's fine now, thanks.

NET: No problem.

STEPHEN: Sorry I didn't recognise you at first.

FRANCES: Hello.

There's a pause.

GARY: Nice evening?

STEPHEN: Yes.

FRANCES: Yes.

GARY: Have a meal?

STEPHEN: Yes. We had a place recommended to us. And it was wonderful. Wasn't it?

FRANCES: Yes. Wonderful.

GARY: We went to one of those clubs you were asking about.

FRANCES *looks at* STEPHEN.

STEPHEN (*not wanting to pursue this*): Right. Drinks. (*As the waitress approaches. Then to* EDWARD:) How about you? What have you been up to?

EDWARD: I had a meal. (*Of* NET.) We had a meal. Quite local, I think. Quite genuine food, I think.

GARY: Nothing like genuine food is what I say, eh Minna? Minna's falling asleep on us.

ADRIAN *returns.*

Adrian, I think Minna's desperate for you to take her to bed.

ADRIAN (*settles with his drink*): Cheers.

FRANCES: Gary was telling us you went to a club. How was that?

ADRIAN: OK.

GARY: It was very naughty.

ADRIAN: It wasn't a club, it was a garage.

GARY: Adrian's decided all Bangkok is actually a garage.

NET: Maybe garage. Many clubs in Bangkok garage once upon a time.

FRANCES: But entertaining nevertheless.

GARY: That's right.

FRANCES: Did your friends enjoy it or did they come with the club?

GARY: We all had a good time, eh chaps?

FRANCES: And have you been to a club as well, Edward?

EDWARD: No.

GARY: But he's got a nice surprise coming later, eh Edward?

EDWARD: There's been a misunderstanding.

FRANCES: Oh?

GARY: That's not what I would have called it. (*To* NET:) You tell them.

Embarrassed a little in front of FRANCES, NET *is silent.*

Tell them! He's fixed Edward up for later.

EDWARD: He hasn't. It's a mistake. He, Net's kindly . . . but, I think what it is, is that women here are not counted for as much. It's not a political attitude, as such, but religious as far as – which is political, of course – is that women are seen as an earlier incarnation, I think that's at the root of it, in Buddhist terms. I don't think Net, I think it was intended as a kindness.

FRANCES: You're saying it wouldn't happen in England?

EDWARD: I don't think it's so likely women would be given as presents. (*Pointed.*) These ladies are presents, apparently.

GARY: Absolutely. They came with bows and everything.

NET: I'm sorry, Edward, if I make bad idea.

EDWARD: Don't worry. No harm done.

FRANCES: Fine. (*To* ADRIAN:) Your present's fallen asleep.

NET (*to* EDWARD): Net thought nice idea for his friend.

EDWARD: Don't worry.

FRANCES: Have you spoken to her?

ADRIAN: She doesn't really speak English.

FRANCES: That figures.

STEPHEN: Anyway.

FRANCES: If there's anything worse than the taste of the tea, it's the taste in my mouth.

EDWARD: Anyway, I think I will . . .

FRANCES: I'll walk up with you.

STEPHEN: Do you want me to come up?

FRANCES: So what was it then? A sex show?

ADRIAN: Yeah.

FRANCES: What sort? Animals?

ADRIAN: No.

FRANCES: No. Just women treated like animals.

ADRIAN: There were men as well.

STEPHEN: This is Fran's hobby-horse, I'm afraid.

FRANCES: What do you mean afraid?

STEPHEN: I'm just warning them.

FRANCES: And so: you sat and watched couples having sex?

ADRIAN: Yes.

FRANCES: Was that erotic?

ADRIAN: No, it was a bit like watching a swimming lesson.

GARY: That's exactly what it was like.

FRANCES: But you watched anyway?

STEPHEN: Fran . . .

GARY: What's your point here, love?

FRANCES: Just curious.

GARY: So were we.

FRANCES: And you took your lady friends?

GARY: Yeah, they came.

FRANCES: Wasn't that odd?

GARY: Lot of couples there. All ages. Americans, Aussies, Germans, all sorts.

FRANCES: A big garage.

GARY: It wasn't a garage.

STEPHEN: I think we should go to bed . . . Fran . . .

EDWARD: Yes, if you'll excuse me as well, I think I'll . . .

FRANCES: So let me get this straight: you went to a club, with these women, and you watched couples having sex? Is that right?

GARY: Yeah we did. It wasn't just fucking. There were novelty acts, weren't there? (*To* ADRIAN.)

ADRIAN: That's right, a woman expelled ping pong balls into a glass of water.

GARY: Except she couldn't do it!

FRANCES (*genuinely lost*): Sorry, what?

GARY: She had ping pong balls up her and she aimed them at a glass of water.

FRANCES: Christ. (*A beat.*) Why?

GARY: I don't know. It was a laugh. She kept missing. It was a laugh.

FRANCES: What was?

GARY: What she was doing. She laughed. We all laughed. Minna laughed. Malee laughed. It wasn't very clever, but she had a go, and you could reload her . . . yeh? . . . so that was fun.

FRANCES (*disgusted*): Oh right.

GARY: It was actually pretty harmless. You know: no one died. No one complained.

FRANCES: I bet.

GARY: That's all right, then.

FRANCES: Was this free entertainment? The ping pong show?

GARY: No, actually, they're doing very well out of it: ten quid a throw.

FRANCES: You paid ten pounds to watch a woman insert ping pong balls into her vagina?

GARY: And aim them at a glass of water. Yeah. Or maybe that was free and we paid to watch the humping. Or maybe the humping was free and we paid to watch the ping pong balls, or five quid each. Who knows? It's a mystery. You're very quiet.

STEPHEN (*thinks* GARY *is speaking to him*): What? No, I just . . . (*Shrugs.*) What can . . .

GARY: Not you. Adrian.

ADRIAN: Yeah.

GARY: You laughed.

ADRIAN: Yeah, I laughed.

NET: You see, I think pretty girls very important for Thailand. Not rich country – like London – many people have empty stomach . . . so tourist very good. These girls come Bangkok make lot baht no problem: Tourist happy, girl happy, family happy, Thailand happy.

FRANCES: I see. Are you married?

NET: Net married, yes.

FRANCES: Would you let your wife sell herself?

NET: My wife? Not so pretty. (*He beams.*) I think nobody buy. (*Small chuckles.* FRANCES *weary.*)

FRANCES: Yeah.

STEPHEN: Come on Frances, you've made your point.

FRANCES: No I haven't actually! Christ! You, men, seem to arrive here and reveal this, because it's available, this great underbelly of . . . it's as if suddenly you kick off your shoes and there are hooves and these great phalluses.

GARY: Don't keep mine in my shoes.

FRANCES: Oh fuck off.

GARY: Whoo!

FRANCES: Yes, whoo! It's so ugly and it's nothing to do with Bangkok, with Thailand, that's the point . . . What's happening here, it's to do with us.

GARY: Does anybody understand this because I don't?

ADRIAN: I think she's asking you to go outside and put a ribbon around your prick and charge people to look at it.

GARY: What?

FRANCES: No. I'm not saying that.

EDWARD: It's the Americans, they made this place into one big Rest and Recreation Zone. They spread Thailand's legs and the rest of the West has visited her ever since. That's what Frances is talking about.

FRANCES: Don't tell me, please, what I'm trying to say.

EDWARD: Oh I thought that was your . . . sorry, what were you . . . anyway it's true about, you don't get two million prostitutes from nowhere . . . What was your point? I'm sorry: I wasn't . . .

There's a pause. FRANCES *doesn't respond.* NET *has been whispering in* MALEE's *ear for some seconds. She nods.*

NET: My friends, I think girls want to get home before too late. I can take them in minibus.

GARY: That's all right, we can arrange a taxi.

NET: No problem.

ADRIAN: Great, do that.

GARY: What: him run them home?

ADRIAN: Yeah.

GARY: I think a few questions have to be asked here.

ADRIAN: Yeah?

GARY: I do. (*Doesn't ask them.*)

FRANCES: It is the power of the erection, a man with an erection loses the capacity to think or hear. He loses the capacity to speak coherently, or act with any sense of others, of a morality, everything gives way to the demands of the penis . . . take me there, put me here, fly me six thousand miles, get me out, get me up . . .

STEPHEN (*over this*): Frances, that's enough.

FRANCES (*dogged*): Talk about a sanctuary of pricks . . . you know that don't you, that Bangkok has a shrine dedicated to your genitals!

GARY (*over this*): I'm going to laugh, what a crease up. Beats the ping pong balls.

ADRIAN: Shut up, Gary.

GARY: Not until she does. It's not my fault she hasn't got a willy.

NET: We go now.

EDWARD: Yes. And me.

STEPHEN: Come on, Frances.

FRANCES: Please. Stop doing that. Stop being embarrassed for me.

GARY (*to* MALEE): See you around then. Here, take this. (*He presses some money into her hands.*) Give us a kiss then. (*They kiss.*) So. All right? See you then.

ADRIAN (*simultaneous with* GARY's *valedictions*): OK? (*To* MINNA:) Sleep tight. (*He, too, gives her money. She raises her hands in a prayer of thanks. Then* FRANCES *comes across to the two girls.*)

FRANCES: I'd like you to have this and this. (*She hands them both more cash and then pulls her bracelet off. To* ADRIAN:) Which one was crying out in your bedroom all afternoon? Or was it both of them?

ADRIAN: I wasn't in my room this afternoon.

A beat while ADRIAN *and* FRANCES *look at each other.*

GARY: It was Malee.

FRANCES: Malee?

MALEE *looks up.* FRANCES *gives her the bracelet.*

I want you to be given something without having to get on your back for it. (*To* MALEE:) Take it. (MALEE *very grateful.*) No, it's my pleasure.

STEPHEN: I gave you that bracelet.

FRANCES: Well now I've given it to Malee. She entertained you this afternoon as well. Now you've paid for it. (STEPHEN *is fantastically embarrassed.*) I'm going to get some air. There's no air in here. I'll see you upstairs. (*She exits.*)

EDWARD: Goodnight. Net, goodnight, I'll see you I expect.

NET: I ring tomorrow, Edward. Sorry about . . .

EDWARD (*dismissing*): Finish.

NET (*smiles*): OK. Finish.

EDWARD: OK. 'Night. (*To* MINNA *and* MALEE.) 'Night.

NET *and* MINNA *and* MALEE *go out.*

'Night. (*To* STEPHEN, GARY *and* ADRIAN.)

Mumbled goodnights from the trio who remain in the litter of the evening. Then a long pause.

STEPHEN: Sorry about that. She's very sensitive. I don't know, we saw a lot of prostitutes tonight and I think . . . it's understandable in a way. Some of them are just children. Our son's nearly seven. Some of them didn't look much older although I'm sure they are, it's the features, all so delicate. She gets very angry about things for some reason. She's not even a feminist. She has to work with a lot of men and she's . . . (*Quite friendly with them.*)

GARY: What did she mean about this afternoon?

STEPHEN: Oh she was, it was because we could hear. The walls aren't exactly . . . we could hear something through the walls. She was just making a point. (*A beat.*) You know.

GARY: Quite the detectives, aren't we?

STEPHEN: They are very thin walls. Doesn't leave much to the imagination.

ADRIAN: And you thought we were all in there, did you? A foursome?

STEPHEN: We didn't spend a lot of time speculating.

GARY: I'd say your Mrs has a few problems.

STEPHEN: Oh, I don't think . . .

ADRIAN: Nor does Gary: think.

GARY: Bought a tee shirt then, eh?

STEPHEN: Yes, it was really cheap. But still: supposed to be a good label, isn't it?

GARY *manages to make his silence a disapproving one.*

Anyway, I quite like it, quite cool. (*Pause.*) Do you know if the silk's any good here? (*Thai silk is world famous.*)

GARY: So they say.

STEPHEN: I think it's supposed to be. I'd like to buy Fran a silk dress or something. I think a lot of it's attention, asking for attention. I'm always up to my eyes at home, really choked up with work, never stops and it's quite difficult to remember to . . . Fran works, but obviously . . . they kick people out of my company: it's quite ruthless. (*Laughs.*) I don't think there's much chance of them kicking me out, but I suppose that's the point. I thought a silk dress or something like that would, I've already had tee shirts and things.

ADRIAN: Yeah, you should buy her a dress.

STEPHEN: I think it would be a good idea. I'll have to guess the size. Or I could have a look inside one of her dresses. (*Prompt mode.*) Sounded like a pretty uh explicit show this evening?

ADRIAN: Well it wasn't subtle.

STEPHEN: Were they actually doing it?

ADRIAN: Oh yes.

STEPHEN (*impressed*): Christ! And this was the place you had recommended?

GARY: One of the places, yeh. Listen: go! Go to one. You're so desperate I can smell it.

STEPHEN: I'm not desperate. I must confess I am curious. And I'd feel as if I'd missed something if I had come all this way and not just had a look. But it's impossible – Christ! Even you must see that.

GARY: You could arrange it.

STEPHEN: Impossible! You're joking!

GARY: Say you've got an evening meeting or something.

STEPHEN: No. It's a nice thought. What would you pay, do you know?

GARY: Dunno. Not much.

STEPHEN: It's academic, anyway.

GARY: Sort it out! Come out with us! You'd have a field day.

STEPHEN: Bedtime! (*Pause.*) If by some fluke I did work something out, I'd be able to tag along with you guys?

GARY: Go for it.

STEPHEN *exits*.

GARY: There are some fucked-up people.

ADRIAN: Go to bed, Gary.

GARY: Is this going to happen every time I want to bring somebody back to the room?

ADRIAN: I expect so.

GARY: I think I'll get another room.

ADRIAN: Fine.

GARY: Loads of people checked out today. I'm going to ask.

ADRIAN: I said OK.

GARY: Don't worry, I'll pay the difference.

ADRIAN: Right.

GARY: Anyway: don't fancy not being able to fart without somebody cataloguing it through the wall, so . . . (*Takes a swig of beer, pulls a face.*) Flat. Shall I tell you the nicest person in the room tonight. This is the truth: Malee. She wasn't dim, you know. She was actually very nice. She was perfectly happy, staying. (*He gets up.*) I'm definitely going to see about another room, first thing tomorrow. Definitely. And I tell you something else for nothing, the difference between us, I thank fuck every day I'm not in the middle classes.

GARY *exits*. ADRIAN *sits with his scotch*. FRANCES *reappears*.

ADRIAN: He's gone upstairs.

She comes towards him, sits down.

FRANCES: You know I thought it was you, this afternoon.

ADRIAN: It could have been.

FRANCES: But it wasn't. Yes it could have been. I'd made this decision, based on nothing at all, an impression, that you wouldn't be casual. And then I thought there he is being casual and I was so disappointed. And anyway. Because somehow over the past few days, at Ayuthya, I'd just thought to every rule there is an exception.

ADRIAN: Where did you go just then?

FRANCES: I'd meant to walk but the streets frighten me. Then I went to the pool, I wanted to dip my feet, but there's a dog . . . it must be a guard dog, I expect . . . so: all a bit abortive.

ADRIAN: We could walk together.

FRANCES: How could you accept a girl as a present?

ADRIAN: So many questions.

FRANCES: I know why anyway. Would you have slept with her?

ADRIAN: I don't know.

FRANCES: It made me so uncomfortable this afternoon, Stephen lying on the bed, enthralled, by the performance.

ADRIAN: Yes.

FRANCES: No, not because of Stephen. I used to listen to this couple above me, at night – I'm talking about in London, years ago – and they used to have sex all the time. Great long loud sessions, really long and really loud and I used to lie in the dark and strain to listen, to hear them, screw up my eyes to catch the whole performance and imagine it: and my face used to go so hot . . . I remember that sensation: the sense of my face going hot, and straining to hear and these great groans and gasps and cries. You'd see them in the day time – this girl was perfectly ordinary, honestly, you wouldn't have given her a second look . . . a quiet hello, she'd be gone, and I'd know she has these fantastic orgasms. And I remember waking up one night and – being woken by this familiar noise – and straining to hear and my face going hot and then realising it wasn't them, it was a baby, it was a baby half crying and it was Christopher, my son, and we weren't even in the same flat any more by this time and I'd woken, hardly woken, and made myself come to the sound of my son crying, waiting for me to feed him. I've been staring at the pool and it's black and I've been trying to remember that room, what it looked like: the room underneath the couple. And I can't. Where does it belong, our fantasy world? Do you know?

ADRIAN: No.

FRANCES: I don't want to despise it but I don't know where it belongs. Because here, it's here isn't it? Out in the open. And it's terrible. And it's terrible bottled up.

She's at the table. ADRIAN *touches her. A beat.*

I want you to know there's no possibility of anything happening between us. I just want that to be clear.

ADRIAN: OK.

FRANCES: You don't say enough. I don't know who I'm talking to.

ADRIAN: Then I'll talk non stop from now on. OK?

FRANCES: OK. So take me for this walk.

They exit.

ACT TWO

Scene One

A massage parlour.
NET *has brought* GARY *and* STEPHEN *to a massage parlour.* NET *clearly has some arrangement with the proprietor.*

NET: My friends, this is Mr Harry. He is boss of Massage Parlour. Best Massage Parlour Bangkok.

HARRY (*shrugs but immodest*): Maybe.

NET (*to* HARRY): These are my friends. Mr Gary and Mr Stephen.

Everyone shakes hands, STEPHEN *distracted by the women.* NET *then begins to speak in Thai, but* GARY *quickly interrupts.*

GARY: Hey, talk in English!

NET (*easily*): Sure. No problem. Just explaining to Harry this first time in Bangkok and massage parlour.

HARRY (*nodding*): First time!

GARY: That's right. So let's get on with it, eh?

This parlour, typically, has a viewing area from which a number of girls can be inspected, behind glass, and apparently oblivious to the attentions of their prospective clients. They wear bikinis and a tag with a number on.

NET: Sure. No problem. (*He shepherds* STEPHEN *to where he can view the girls.*) Don't worry, they can't see you. This is a one-way mirror. Choose! You choose and you tell Harry the number.

HARRY: You can ask me about girls.

NET: Yes, ask him about each one, he can tell you anything.

HARRY: Just ask! Number 12: number 6, any number: I tell you everything.

NET: They can't see you. Look carefully: choose. You tell Harry: Harry call their number. Girls meet you in the cubicle. Each cubicle has a tub – all clean – a tub, lots of suds, girls make lots of suds, and then you bath, they bath you: very nice. No one wears any clothes, very nice. Have a drink, all air conditioned –

HARRY: Whole place air-conditioned by the way.

NET: – then you come through to the place where you have your massage. And also here is a bed to relax afterwards. The massage . . . lots of suds . . . not done with the hands only, but with the whole body –

HARRY (*beams*): Called B Course!

NET: Yes . . . this is called B Course. Hard if you are doing the massage. Not so hard if you are the lucky one underneath. You pay for the massage now. Choose first, then pay, of course! Maybe you want other things after your B Course: some special service. Maybe not. This is possible. This you pay for – you must negotiate with your girl at the time.

HARRY: All my girls show card stamped every week at VD clinic. This rule for me, no stamp: no work. (*Checks with NET, who nods authoritatively.*) Very strict.

NET: OK? So now: choose. Take your time. We leave you. Girls can't see you. One-way mirror. Like window shopping.

GARY: And we get special price, yeah? Coming with you?

NET: Sure. No problem. Net get friends special price. Choose first. Talk money after. Don't worry. But Net must go now. Back to hotel. Work work. (*He and HARRY make to exit.*)

STEPHEN: Hang on, Net. Hang on a minute. (*He fishes out a bank note and gives it to NET.*)

NET (*accepting it*): Very kind.(*He exits.*)

STEPHEN (*excited, incredulous, excited*): They really do have numbers! It's staggering! How much do you think they'll charge us, you know, for the massage? And then if – I have to know how much in toto – because otherwise I may have to cash another traveller's cheque which is fine but will take explaining away. (*Looks.*) It is actually staggering.

GARY: Pay with plastic.

STEPHEN: What? Credit card?

GARY: It said they took it.

STEPHEN: What would they charge you for? What would they call it?

GARY: You wouldn't be the first. There's probably some code, something dead diplomatic: get your Visa bill: Fuck – forty quid.

STEPHEN: You think forty, do you?

GARY: I've no idea. But I know who I'm going to choose: Come in Number 7. Your time is up, up, up.

STEPHEN (*looking for her*): Number 7?

GARY: I don't know why you gave Net anything. He'll get a cut anyway. You fart in this place, somebody gets a percentage.

STEPHEN: Perhaps. But it's an investment. I don't want him, I want him to be discreet, you know, and not . . .

GARY: Although it has to be said that 3 is extremely tasty.

STEPHEN (*looking for her*): 3?

GARY: Oh 3 is definitely a one to watch.

STEPHEN: Why do they call it B Course?

GARY: I dunno. You should have asked Net.

STEPHEN: I've got to be back by 5.30 and pick up Fran's dress. I really have.

GARY: I want to see those cards.

STEPHEN: Yes, that sounded reassuring. 3 looks quite Western.

GARY: I'm bagging 3.

STEPHEN: One of them's knitting! 12!

GARY: 12? Oh yeah.

STEPHEN: White bikini.

GARY: Yeah.

STEPHEN: Do you really think they can't see us? 7 is nice, isn't she? Looks quite intelligent.

GARY: Well she's reading. What has intelligence got to do with anything? Are you going to play scrabble?

STEPHEN: I will probably just have the massage, I expect.

GARY: Reckon!

STEPHEN: I'm glad we're doing it this way round.

GARY: What way?

STEPHEN: Well, here first and then to the

clothes place, because otherwise all I mean is obviously we're going to be quite clean, aren't we, with the bath and what have you, which might seem a bit odd, given the weather, but if we – this way round we're bound to get quite, I'm going through three shirts a day.

GARY: Thank you Sherlock Holmes.

STEPHEN: Listen: my wife is no fool.

GARY: So you had a massage. What's your wife doing?

STEPHEN: She's gone to the Grand Palace, look at some Buddha or other, an emerald Buddha I think, plus Thai dancing. I think she's hoping to write some sort of article. (*Distracted.*) Actually she's nice, too.

GARY: Where?

STEPHEN: With the gold chain. Next to 7.

GARY: Oh yeah. (*Looks.*) Yeah. Well, have two together.

STEPHEN (*dismissive*): Oh . . .

GARY: Rub different bits. You look so excited!

STEPHEN: I suppose I am. It's an experience, isn't it? I love massages anyway.

HARRY   *reappearing*): Well, my friends, very difficult to choose, eh?

STEPHEN: Very.

HARRY: Want my advice? 7 very good.

GARY: What about 3?

HARRY: 3 also excellent. Tell the truth: all special girls. 3 half not Thai. Maybe American. Very young.

STEPHEN: I like 8.

HARRY: 8 also special. Good for round the world.

STEPHEN: Round the world? What's that?

HARRY (*laughs*): Round the world? Just ask. Say round the world. 8 understand. Then enjoy.

STEPHEN: Well OK, I think 8, then.

HARRY: For you, 8; and for you, sir?

GARY: 3.

HARRY: 3? OK.

Goes to microphone, or off, and bawls out the number.

8, 3, Beht! Sam! (*Then turns to* STEPHEN *and* GARY:) You pay me nine hundred baht each now.

GARY: Is that our special price?

HARRY: All special price for friends.

Two girls appear in bikinis. They carry towels. Number 8 and Number 3.

Who was Number 8?

STEPHEN: Me.

HARRY *jerks his head at* 8 . . . *who comes to* STEPHEN. GARY *walks towards* 3.

GARY: Hello 3.

HARRY (*smiles*): American Express?

Scene Two

ADRIAN's *bedroom.*
  ADRIAN *and* FRANCES *alone, early afternoon.*

FRANCES: I don't just want to make love. What present would you get from Thailand for a seven-year-old?

ADRIAN: Is this your son?

FRANCES: He likes hittings things. And guns. No, actually he can be very sensitive. He has a real problem with the loo. He doesn't go. For days at a time. I think I must have done something very wrong at one time. Do you have guilt? It goes round me like blood. It's a family characteristic. And I've passed it on. Anyway, what should I get him? Someone tried to sell me a knife at the market. He would have loved that.

ADRIAN: We don't have to make love at all. We can go and look at the Emerald Buddha. We can buy your son his present.

FRANCES: Do you know what happens in Dante to the lustful? They wander around for ever. That's their fate. The roving eye can never stop roving. Pretty good, eh? The flatterers are stuck in manure, the lustful wander and the seducers are scourged.

ADRIAN: What would we be? Lust or seducers?

FRANCES: Oh, lust. That's mutual.

ADRIAN: Good: I've always travelled. I'm not so keen on getting whipped.

FRANCES: Do you go in for holiday romance? Don't answer that. This morning there was a condom in the bathroom. It must have come up through the plumbing or something. I hate those things. A friend of mine had a problem with their drains a couple of years ago. They live in the country and it's all fairly primitive. I know I'm talking too much, but I'm nervous and this is my first rove, as they say, scrub that, it's a lie, nevertheless relatively unroved, so . . . they live in the country, problem with drains and they call in the thing, the person, whatever board it would be, the Water Board, whoever, no the drain clearers, and this chap arrives with all the equipment and Jan took him to the cover outside and he lifted it up, they were chatting all the while, and inside the cover, underneath, blocking the drain, was about a year's worth of their waste in all its glory, this jamboree bag of Durex and Tampax mixed up with everything else. And Jan said they both stared at this . . . this (*Shrugs.*) and then she went back indoors and, well she did nothing, that's not the point, the point is that the effort to appear civilised . . . is so thin, is such a sham.

ADRIAN: To answer your question, no I don't. (FRANCES *is confused.*) Holiday romances. Go in for them.

FRANCES: Do you think Stephen has flings? (*She asks in a way that encourages the negative.*)

ADRIAN: I expect so.

FRANCES: Actually, I don't think so. I think there's bravado. I really don't think he does.

ADRIAN: If you were painting a room, lots of rooms in a house, what colour would you paint them?

FRANCES: This is a game, isn't it? What's it called? Where you say: if I were a room what room would I be? What flower?

ADRIAN: No, I'm serious. I've bought a house and I need to paint it. It needs decorating. And I want it to be . . . I don't know . . .

FRANCES: What?

ADRIAN: Somewhere nice. I've bought all the magazines. My daughter has ideas, of course.

FRANCES: I didn't know you had a daughter. Have you got a wife?

ADRIAN: No wife.

FRANCES: How old's your daughter? What's her name?

ADRIAN: Jeannie. She's twenty.

FRANCES: Jeannie.

ADRIAN: I think she thinks she's in love with Gary.

FRANCES: Gary as in Gary here?

ADRIAN: That's right.

FRANCES: Oh.

ADRIAN: That's one of the reasons I brought him with me.

FRANCES: I see.

ADRIAN: Not only that reason.

FRANCES: And does Gary think he's in love with your daughter?

ADRIAN: I haven't asked him. Judging from his performance to date I'd say if he is he's keeping it a closely guarded secret.

FRANCES: Can I assume you're not delighted about this love affair? Is it a love affair?

ADRIAN: I'm not delighted, no.

FRANCES: You're being quite calculating bringing him with you, aren't you?

ADRIAN: Maybe.

FRANCES: Oh yes, because everything he does can be used against him . . . very ingenious. Does he know you know all about this?

ADRIAN: I doubt it.

FRANCES: That explains a lot.

ADRIAN: Really?

FRANCES: When I first met you, I suppose I tarred you with the same brush, except I didn't of course, but I couldn't quite work out the double act, now I see it was just a protective dad, perfectly clear.

ADRIAN: That's it.

FRANCES: I'm not sure if I like it much.

ADRIAN: I'm not asking you to. I love my daughter. I'm not going to let some jerk mess up her life. It's not Gary in particular, it's Garys in general.

FRANCES: What does Jeannie's mother have to say about all this?

ADRIAN: I've no idea. We don't see her.

FRANCES: This is going wrong.

ADRIAN: Yes.

FRANCES: I've been fantasising, I suppose it is fantasising, yes, anyway, about falling in love with you. Now, I'm not sure whether this is because in my mind, because of this guilt business, I have to convince myself I'm in love before I can get into the bed with you, or whether it's because I'm in Bangkok and you are the only good thing to have emerged, along with the Reclining Buddha, or because you seem to listen to me, or what . . . I don't know . . . (*She touches him.*) Is there a woman at home?

ADRIAN: Yes.

FRANCES: Right.

ADRIAN: Well, there's a husband in your luggage.

FRANCES: Declared.

ADRIAN: I've declared a woman at home and a daughter.

FRANCES: It's just I want to think there's one relationship I can have in my life which is honest, even if it's only for a few days, I want to think I can say everything without fear.

ADRIAN: Well you can.

FRANCES: And so can you.

ADRIAN: Right.

They can't think of anything to say. They chuckle.

Who's G?

FRANCES: G?

ADRIAN: You had a handkerchief on the boat, on the walk, the other day, it was initialled . . . G . . . (FRANCES *produces the handkerchief.*) That's it.

FRANCES: I don't know. (*Pause.*) Honestly. (*Pause.*) Do you really want to know?

ADRIAN: Yes.

FRANCES: It was given to me by a lover.

ADRIAN: So you do know.

FRANCES: His name didn't begin with G either. Really. He said it was given to him, too. And the person, woman, who gave it to him wasn't a G either, so . . .

ADRIAN: Glad I asked.

FRANCES: You don't believe me, do you?

ADRIAN: I do! I do.

FRANCES: He gave it to me when I was crying about something, to do with him or us or, it was hopeless and I was crying and he gave me his hankie and off we went identifying it or failing to just like now and I've always treasured it because I think of it as being handed on from lover to lover for tears etc.

ADRIAN: Etc.

FRANCES: I should give it to you.

ADRIAN: Oh, are you anticipating I'll cry?

FRANCES: I'm anticipating etc.

ADRIAN: OK. Thank you.

And they embrace for the first time.

Scene Three.

The coffee shop.
    NET *brings* EDWARD *cheese on toast.*

NET: Cheese on toast.

EDWARD: Thank you Net.

    NET *stays.*

NET: OK?

EDWARD (*eating*): Ngh. (*Yes.*)

NET: Want ketchup?

EDWARD (*eating*): Ngh. (*No.*)

NET: Today weather not so good.

EDWARD: No.

NET: Some days Buddha sunbathe all day, some days he take big bath.

EDWARD: That's right.

NET: Today Buddha have big bath. Net get very wet. Mr Edward get very wet?

EDWARD: No.

NET: No kid?

EDWARD: Mr Edward stay in hotel.

NET: All day?

EDWARD: All day.

NET (*impressed*): No kid.

EDWARD: Net, does no one mind you talking to me?

NET: No.

EDWARD: Shouldn't you be working?

NET: Edward my customer. No problem.

EDWARD *eats*.

So: what my friend do today? Read books! (*He seems to find this quite funny.*)

EDWARD: Yes, I did, that's right. Why's that funny?

NET: Just funny.

EDWARD: Why?

NET: No, just Net wonder maybe Edward have girlfriend in room but you don't tell Net maybe, maybe not like other men who go up and down in lift with Thai girl, slap bottom, make big joke, big noise. Edward quiet, go up and down in lift by yourself but still Thai girl in room. I just wonder.

EDWARD: Are there only two types of men? Those who admit to having girls in their rooms and those who don't?

NET: Sorry. Don't follow.

EDWARD: Well, no matter. I was actually reading a book about Thai politics.

NET (*unimpressed*): Ach.

EDWARD: Your army is very powerful.

NET: Very powerful.

EDWARD: Too powerful, my book says.

NET (*unimpressed*): Ach.

EDWARD: What does Net think?

NET: Not so interested in politics, to tell truth.

EDWARD: You should be. You can change things.

NET: Net change things? Ha! Not possible. Always say: Buddha can change world; Net can change tyre.

EDWARD: Not true. Really. Not true.

NET: Net think true. No problem. What you do tonight: more reading!

EDWARD: A walk perhaps, I don't know. Depends on the weather. Maybe a walk.

NET: Tomorrow night, Net not work, is Edward's last night or not?

EDWARD: Yes, that's right.

NET: OK. Maybe tomorrow night. Net show Edward Thai boxing?

EDWARD: Maybe.

NET: Special evening for my friend. Maybe go Thai boxing then cousin's house watch special film.

EDWARD: Net, really . . .

NET: Understand, Edward not like do anything except maybe look.

EDWARD: That's right.

NET: Still, maybe look at film, same thing. Very sexy film.

EDWARD *points at* NET *and pulls imaginary trigger*. NET *laughs*.

FRANCES *enters, from the lift, if there is one. She sits at another table. Smiles politely at* EDWARD *and* NET. *They nod greetings.*

OK. Net bring Edward more food?

EDWARD: No thank you.

NET: Net find just sweet for friend. Come straight back. One you like.

EDWARD: Thank you. Kawpkun.

NET: Mai pen rai. (*Goes to* FRANCES;) And for madam?

FRANCES: Iced tea please.

NET: Iced tea.

ADRIAN *enters, again from the lift.*

Want something sir?

ADRIAN: No thanks.

FRANCES: Hello.

ADRIAN: Hello.

FRANCES: Are you going to join me?

ADRIAN: No.

FRANCES: I'm just waiting for Stephen.

ADRIAN: What are you doing tomorrow?

FRANCES: I'm not sure.

ADRIAN: I'd like to take you to dinner tomorrow evening.

EDWARD *can hear all this. He looks at his tablecloth.*

FRANCES: I don't know what we're doing.

ADRIAN (*levelly*): Just you, Frances.

FRANCES (*levelly*): Well I'd like to but obviously I can't if Stephen has already made other arrangements.

ADRIAN: There are only two more days.

FRANCES: There's Hong Kong.

ADRIAN: Let me know about tomorrow.

FRANCES: I will.

He exits. There's a pause. Eventually FRANCES *addresses* EDWARD.

Horrible weather.

EDWARD: Afraid so.

FRANCES: I'd hoped to get out, go to the market, but I couldn't face it. My husband's still out. He's got business today. He'll be drenched. I don't suppose you've seen him?

EDWARD: Sorry, no.

FRANCES: I get a headache in this kind of weather. I had a sleep.

EDWARD: I've been reading a very interesting book. About Thai politics.

FRANCES: Really? And is that, what, is that interesting?

EDWARD: Just makes me so angry. The waste. The exploitation. Mind you, Hong Kong's just as bad. I work in the refugee camps, the Boat People, and I can't get anybody to empty the bins! I can't get bins! Last month, the month before, March, I went to a charity dinner at the golf club, black tie, puddings in the shape of the Island, you know, in the shape of Hong Kong, fifty dishes, and at my table half the people who administrate the camps, OK, and so I brought up this subject of the bins, because they were all there and I was pig sick of writing memos

– I hate memos – I hate bureaucracy. So I just said – 'What about these bins then?'

FRANCES: And what happened?

EDWARD: I got them. I got the bins. Next day. But I also got completely ignored for the rest of the dinner and it was made clear to me I wouldn't get another invitation. Ignorant. Underneath the black ties they're all ignorant bloody apes.

NET *ushers in* STEPHEN *and tea and a dish of something for* EDWARD.

NET: See! (*He's been* STEPHEN*'s guide.*)

STEPHEN: Hello darling, the waiter told me you'd be here.

FRANCES: Hello.

NET: I bring extra cup. Mr Edward enjoy nice sweet things.

EDWARD: Thank you.

STEPHEN, *terribly conscious of* NET, *waits until he has exited before elaborating on his deception.*

STEPHEN: I'm soaked. Am I late? Everybody's fighting for a cab. Madness. I got you a present.

FRANCES: Did you? Can I see? How was the meeting?

STEPHEN: Oh OK. It's something you'll have to try on.

FRANCES: Really?

STEPHEN: Not here.

FRANCES: Right. I didn't get to the market. I got a headache.

STEPHEN: So what did you do? What a drag.

FRANCES: I went to bed.

STEPHEN: Did you sleep it off?

FRANCES: A bit. I feel better now.

GARY *enters.*

GARY: Hi.

STEPHEN: Oh hello. How are you?

GARY: Fine. How are you?

A beat.

STEPHEN: Wet.

GARY: Right. Seen Adrian around?

FRANCES: No.

STEPHEN: I haven't. No.

GARY (*to* EDWARD): Have you?

EDWARD (*compromised*): No I don't think so.

GARY: Fair enough.

STEPHEN *is very uncomfortable.*

STEPHEN: Let's go upstairs and I can show you your present.

FRANCES: Have your tea first, eh?

STEPHEN: Oh yes.

GARY: Well I don't know about anybody else but I'm absolutely shagged out. (*Pause.*) Mmm?(*He looks about mischievously.*)

EDWARD: It's the humidity, I expect.

STEPHEN: Why don't you go on up ahead and try this thing on?

GARY: What's this? (*He massages* STEPHEN's *shoulders.*)

STEPHEN: I've bought Frances a present.

GARY: That's nice. Isn't that nice?

FRANCES: I think so. (*To* STEPHEN:) OK.

STEPHEN: Gary's teasing. He knows what it is. He helped me sort it out.

FRANCES: I wondered what was going on.

GARY: That's right: I'm just winding Stephen up. It's so easy, isn't it?

FRANCES: I will go on up.

STEPHEN: I'll come with you. I'll just gulp down my tea. I might even ask him to send it to the room. (*Hands her the parcel.*) Anyway, hope you like it, my darling.

FRANCES: Thank you. See you in a minute.

She exits. STEPHEN *glowers at* GARY.

GARY: What's the matter?

STEPHEN *refuses to join in.*

Did you think I was going to tell her you'd been around the world?

STEPHEN: Don't Gary, for God's sake, not even as a joke.

STEPHEN *is half-terrified of being found out, half-delighted at his exploits.*

GARY: Just geeing you up.

STEPHEN: Well don't

GARY: My lips are sealed, said the tart to the elephant.

NET *returns.*

NET: Tea for sir, (*Going on to* EDWARD:) also coffee for my friend. (*To* GARY:) Did you want drink, sir?

GARY: Yes, a singha, cold.

NET: Cold beer: singha; no problem.

GARY: If it's not cold I don't want it.

NET: Understand.

GARY: Hey listen: well done this afternoon. We were very impressed, eh Steve?

NET: Thank you. I hope so.

GARY: Oh yeah, brilliant.

STEPHEN (*conscious of* EDWARD): There's no need to . . .

GARY: My friend and I would be very interested in doing some more business with you.

NET: Sure, what kind of business?

GARY: My friend would like to know how much it would cost to have two Thai girlfriends for an evening.

NET: Two girlfriends?

GARY: That's right.

STEPHEN: Gary . . .

NET: Talking about nice girls?

GARY: Very nice.

NET: Very nice girls maybe not too old?

GARY: Very nice young girls.

NET: Which evening? This evening?

GARY: Tomorrow evening? (*Looks at* STEPHEN.) Tomorrow evening? (STEPHEN *doesn't respond, but he's listening.*)

NET: All night?

GARY *looks across, amused, as* STEPHEN *raises his eyes.*

GARY: Probably not.

NET: Still talking about a lot of baht.

STEPHEN (*muttering*): Certificates.

GARY (*hears*): What? (*To* NET:) I think this friend would want to see certificates.

NET: What kind certificates?

GARY: Like this afternoon: no clap.

NET: Understand. No problem. All certificates. Clean girls. Just come up country.

GARY: So how much?

NET: Maybe two thousand baht.

GARY: Come on, we're not thick.

NET: Good price.

GARY: I said two girls not twenty-two.

NET: Twenty-two! Twenty-two many thousand baht! Twenty-two!

GARY: My friend was thinking more in the region of one thousand.

NET: Net sorry but two thousand special price because you friends.

GARY: I see. It's a shame because I could have put some more business your way because I might also want some company tomorrow.

NET: So talking about altogether three nice girls?

GARY: That's right.

NET: I go get singha beer for my friend also speak (*Mimes telephone call.*) Come back with special price. Like today: always special price.

EDWARD, GARY, STEPHEN *alone.* EDWARD *transfixed by the negotiations,* STEPHEN *too.*

GARY: I think we would expect to pay two thousand for all three, eh?

STEPHEN: I have to go on upstairs.

GARY: What do you want to do, then?

STEPHEN: Look, I'm not sure I . . . I really have to, Fran'll wonder where, what I'm playing at.

GARY: You could help us. (EDWARD). He could help us.

EDWARD: I'm sorry?

GARY: Don't pretend you weren't listening. Your ears were flapping like (*Looks to* STEPHEN:) I thought he was going to take off.

EDWARD: I think that's rather an exaggeration.

GARY (*cutting in*): The fact is the guy obviously fancies you or something the way he oils all over you – if he tossed you you'd be a salad. Does he?

EDWARD: Don't be . . .

GARY (*cutting in*): That's my guess – a shirt lifter – beat him down for us, do us a favour.

EDWARD: If you want to buy women, that's your business. Don't involve me.

STEPHEN: I really do have to go.

GARY: Come on, I've got to think it's a bargain. I can't bear paying top whack. Try and get him down to one thousand baht. I'll come to you for my fillings. 'Cause he took us to a massage place this afternoon and I'm sure we paid too much.

EDWARD: Net did?

GARY: Yeah.

EDWARD: If you really want my opinion and to be quite honest with you I hate the way you behave, I despise it actually.

GARY: You can't say fairer than that.

EDWARD (EDWARD *is flustered*): I despise your mock, your mock, your facetiousness.

GARY: My mock, my mock, my facetiousness?

EDWARD: Because Net is a good man compromised by his circumstances. Because otherwise he wouldn't have to procure for you, he wouldn't have to bring you cold beer or be insulted by you.

GARY: Who's insulted him? I haven't insulted him. I said he fancies you. Is that an insult?

STEPHEN: I think we should just drop this, I wasn't really serious.

NET *reappears.*

NET: OK, Net have very good deal. Special rate for friends. Cold singha beer for my friend, no charge.

GARY: Lovely.

NET: For these girls tomorrow night come 8.00 leave 12.00.

GARY: Cinderellas.

NET (*doesn't understand*): All clean girls. One thousand and five hundred baht. Best price I can do. Five hundred now, one thousand tomorrow.

GARY: What's that? Fifty quid?

STEPHEN: Yes.

GARY: That would be say thirty-five you: fifteen me. What do you reckon?

STEPHEN: I'll have to think about it. I haven't even, I'll even have to cash a traveller's cheque, I'll have to . . . (*Hesitating.*) It'll be quite awkward, whichever. (*To* GARY:) Thirty-five/fifteen, it's not exactly properly . . . (*He thinks it's an uneven split.*)

GARY: We'll give you twelve hundred baht now, cash.

STEPHEN (*protesting*): I haven't.

GARY: Yes or no?

NET: Twelve hundred cash now?

GARY: Now.

NET: OK. For Net nothing, but OK because all friends here. Cash now please.

GARY: Great. Magic. I've got four hundred, I think. Five hundred, five-fifty. What have you got?

STEPHEN: Not enough, I've only got, I've got five hundred. I'll have to cash a traveller's cheque, I can't come down again tonight. Shit, this is taking ages.

GARY: Lend us two hundred baht. (*To* EDWARD.)

EDWARD: I'm sorry, I can't.

GARY: Course you can, come on. Lend Stephen two hundred baht until the morning. Otherwise you're going to cause a real domestic rift, real problems. Two hundred baht.

STEPHEN: I can pay you at breakfast.

EDWARD: I'm sorry, I can't, I said. It goes completely against the grain. I don't think I can actually help you to exploit women, girls. It would be ridiculous.

GARY (*of* EDWARD): You see. He's worse than us, because all we want to do is fuck them. He wants them to kiss his arse. He wants them to be his mission. It's like school. It's like the fucking black babies. See your little flag go up the stairs. That's what we had at school . . . a little chart with stairs and a picture of God at the top. Each time you gave a penny, a flag with your name went up a stair. (*Disgust.*) Did you have those? 'Edward, you have given five bob to the black babies. Here's your flag up at the top of the ladder. Go straight to heaven, do not pass go.'

NET: No problem. Net take one thousand now, two hundred tomorrow. No trouble, please.

EDWARD: Here you are, I'll give you your two hundred baht.

NET: No kid, Mr Edward: tomorrow fine.

EDWARD: Just take it. (*Gives him the two hundred baht.*)

STEPHEN: Honestly, you'll have it back by breakfast.

EDWARD *exits.*

Listen I wonder if I could sign my bill for the tea, and for my wife's? Only I'm cleaned out.

NET, *who's quite disturbed by the unpleasantness, just hands him the bill.*

Thank you.

NET: Tomorrow, girls come reception eight p.m.

STEPHEN: Uh, (*To* GARY:) couldn't we have them sent up to your room? You did say you could work something with . . .

GARY: Yeah, but I've got to check with Adrian he'll lend me his room. Yeah, OK, have them sent up.

NET: Understand. Your room. Eight p.m.

NET *exits.*

STEPHEN: Right. I wish you hadn't tormented that bloke. He's already liable to tell Fran.

GARY: No, he's much too frightened. He'll go to his room and have a wank and *imagine* he's told her.

STEPHEN: I'm glad you're so sure.

GARY: He's frightened we'd make him cry. I keep thinking he's going to anyway.

Well go on then, and see you tomorrow. At the ball, Prince Charming: eight p.m.

Scene Four

The bedroom. FRANCES *and* STEPHEN.

FRANCES: What happened? Where've you been?

STEPHEN: I got talking. Sorry. With Edward.

FRANCES (*guilty*): Oh, what did he say?

STEPHEN (*guilty*): Just on his hobby-horse, I don't know.

FRANCES: I see.

STEPHEN: Gary's right. He thinks – Edward – thinks if you make enough noise about something then you're absolved. If you blame enough people you're let off.

FRANCES: And what: who was he criticising? Gary and Adrian?

STEPHEN: Not Adrian. I mean Adrian wasn't there. Why?

FRANCES: Oh darling, I haven't modelled my dress. Or said thank you. How did you get my size?

STEPHEN: Gary helped. I looked in your blue dress. Is it all right?

FRANCES: It's wonderful. I'm so touched you even, and that it's silk. Let me show you.

Having held up the dress, she begins the process of modelling it.

STEPHEN: Well, you said you wanted silk.

FRANCES: I know I said. I wasn't sure you listened. It's beautiful, Stephen. You never bought me a dress before.

STEPHEN: I've paid for dresses.

FRANCES: Well, there's a difference. How was your meeting?

STEPHEN: Yes, OK. I'll have to go to the main factory tomorrow. To say I've been.

FRANCES: Shall I come?

STEPHEN: If you'd like to.

FRANCES: Would you like me to?

STEPHEN: Yes, of course. We may have to eat with some of them.

FRANCES: Lunch or dinner?

STEPHEN: Perhaps both.

FRANCES: Not both, Stephen.

STEPHEN: Well listen, come with me, have lunch and if they insist on my stopping for supper then you can come back.

FRANCES: Or the other way round.

STEPHEN: Or the other way round, you mean you come later and have supper? Yes fine. Would you prefer that?

FRANCES: Whichever.

STEPHEN: Lunch would be shorter.

(*Kicks of his shoes.*)

FRANCES: That's fine. Whichever you'd like, darling. Although actually I would rather come with you, have lunch and then go off. I still haven't got anything for Christopher.

STEPHEN: You won't be lonely in the evening?

FRANCES: No, I expect I'll join one of the tours. I haven't seen any Thai boxing.

STEPHEN: OK.

FRANCES: Can I wear my new dress?

STEPHEN: Yeah. It's beautiful. You look beautiful.

FRANCES: Thank you.

STEPHEN: You're soft today.

FRANCES: Am I? You're soft, too. (*They embrace.*) And you smell nice.

STEPHEN: What do you mean?

FRANCES: You smell nice!

STEPHEN: Are you teasing me because I'm sweaty or something?

FRANCES: No!

STEPHEN: You're only happy when I'm in the bath.

FRANCES: True.

STEPHEN: I went for a massage today.

They stay embracing, except stiffly.

FRANCES: Oh?

STEPHEN: I was curious.

FRANCES: What sort of massage? I thought you were visiting Mr Thinsa?

STEPHEN: On the way. On the way back. Before I collected your dress I had some time to kill. I went with Gary.

FRANCES: Right.

STEPHEN: That's why I smell clean, I expect. They give you a bath, there's a bath. You should be happy.

FRANCES: A woman gave you this massage, I take it?

STEPHEN: You don't get offered a choice.

FRANCES: And of course if you had been . . .

STEPHEN: It wasn't sexual. I'm not saying I didn't expect it to be. I'm saying it didn't turn out to be sexual. I had a really vigorous massage and that was it. (*Pause.*) I mean, of course it was quite, I'm not pretending it wasn't, the fact is I'm telling you and I didn't have to.

FRANCES: I spent the afternoon with Adrian.

STEPHEN: Meaning?

FRANCES: As we're talking about what we did this afternoon.

STEPHEN: What do you mean you spent the afternoon with him?

FRANCES: What do you mean you had a really vigorous massage?

STEPHEN: Are you serious?

FRANCES: I am, yes.

STEPHEN: Where? Where did it happen, this spending of the afternoon? In here?

FRANCES: No.

STEPHEN: Where then?

FRANCES: Don't get aggressive, Stephen, please.

STEPHEN: Christ.

FRANCES: Please don't.

STEPHEN: It's brilliant, isn't it? Because I go for a massage, which is what thousands of men do when they come to Thailand on holiday. A harmless massage, which I'm meant to be guilty, feel guilty about, have this big confession over and I feel like some sort of pervert – and my wife – because it's practically perverse not to go to one of these places we go to the reclining Buddha and buy silk and take pictures of the squalor and all the painted men lifting up their skirts which is all fine, and all the time my wife is, it's fucking brilliant, isn't it? In this bed, was it? (*He rips the duvet off the bed.*)

FRANCES: I didn't say I went to bed with him. Stephen, if you're going to get agitated I'm going to have to leave the room.

STEPHEN: Yes, do, fuck off, go and see your friend, Adrian. He's old enough to be your father, it's pathetic.

FRANCES: It was actually something I wanted to talk to you about, I thought we could talk about things, what's missing between us, why someone like Adrian could even begin to be a threat, why I can't give you a massage if it's about you want: I like massaging you . . . I keep trying to talk, please talk to me, Stephen. Because just now we were close, weren't we and I was so happy about the dress and now I see it was just something to wrap your afternoon in.

STEPHEN: You think everything will yield to chat, Frances. Well it won't.

FRANCES: OK.

STEPHEN: Because there's no logic.

FRANCES: OK.

STEPHEN: That's all. Particularly for men.

FRANCES: Why particularly for men? (*The ceiling has begun to leak. FRANCES examines it.*) Oh Christ.

STEPHEN: Because you think it has to be love, don't you? Or nothing. There can't be just, but in fact (*Can't tell her.*) – I can't even tell you. I don't think there's anything I can ask you to do. You find a magazine, just photographs, and there's an inquisition.

FRANCES: I just don't happen to think it's on for women to . . .

STEPHEN: Exactly. You won't, when was the last time we had (*Embarrassed*), if I come in your mouth it's like I'm supposed to think it's Christmas. You don't even like our son now. The house is a tip, I can't invite people back because I don't know how, what the place will look like: people get fired or . . . I happen to know

Howard got the Manchester office on the strength of a conversation at a dinner party at their house. You want to think about what it feels like for your wife to tell you she doesn't like your son.

FRANCES: Not very nice, I expect.

STEPHEN: That's right. Not very nice.

FRANCES: This rain is ridiculous. Can't we do anything about that drip, it's driving me . . . (*She shoves the waste bin under the drip. It only serves to exacerbate the noise, and what follows is punctuated by a sporadic beat.*)

STEPHEN: It just doesn't yield to chat.

FRANCES: No.

STEPHEN: Well let me tell you there's a cellar, inside me, inside . . . no, there's, I can't think of a word, it's got things even I don't want to look at and I'm not alone in this and I don't see why I should have to feel, I don't even want to talk about it.

FRANCES: I'm actually missing Christopher very badly today. For the record. I wanted us to call him this evening. I don't like dinner parties, I never did. I never have. Your friends, the people you work with – which is a different thing, it's a farce the – you've said this – 'They invited us so we invite them' that's a farce, Stephen. And you excel in liking what you don't do yourself like tidying up which is OK, but in fact I don't see it – so don't accuse me. I've never left my clothes on the floor: you both do. Women were not born bent double and . . . (*embarrassed*) I've, we discussed this and you said you understood, it feels as if I'm choking, it can feel that and you're never very . . . oh anyway let's have supper shall we or just, not stay in here? The window's leaking as well. Can we call someone? The drains can't cope with all the water: did I tell you there was a condom in the bathroom this morning?

STEPHEN: Yes.

FRANCES: Ugh. I hate those things.

STEPHEN: Frances, you hate rubbers, you hate the cap, you hate the pill.

FRANCES: Yes I do hate those things.

STEPHEN: Just think about it . . . maybe it's something else you hate.

FRANCES: No. I hate those things. Whereas you hate the womb.

STEPHEN: Oh yes, that's right!

FRANCES: Whereas you hate the womb.

STEPHEN: It doesn't get any more true by repeating it.

FRANCES: Whereas you hate the womb Stephen.

STEPHEN: I'm going to have to leave the room, Frances, because otherwise I could hit you, really hit you: not what you think is hitting.

FRANCES: Then leave the room. Or I will.

STEPHEN: OK. (*Going.*) I'll see you later.

FRANCES: Where are you going?

STEPHEN: I don't know. Oh shit, I haven't got any money.

FRANCES: Haven't you? You must have.

STEPHEN: Have you got any cash? Or the traveller's cheques?

FRANCES: Well I've got a bit. I've got the rest of the traveller's cheques. I hope it was the dress which was expensive. (*She goes to her bag.*) Is this enough?

STEPHEN: I expect so, I can't go out without money.

FRANCES: You should take the umbrella. It's in the bathroom. I'll get it.

STEPHEN: It's all right. I'll go.

He exits. FRAN *sits on the bed. He comes back with the umbrella which has been opened to drain off in the bath. He can't work out how to close it. Somehow everything has become slightly comic.*

FRANCES: Let me.

STEPHEN: It's OK. It's a stupid design. (*Fiddles.*) Bloody thing. (*He half closes it.*) I'll see you later.

FRANCES: Stephen, you haven't got your shoes on.

STEPHEN: Where are my shoes?

FRAN *picks them up, goes to him, kneels down and helps him put them on. She's bent down in front of him. She puts his shoes on. She puts her arm around his knees.* STEPHEN *hits her: very hard.*

Scene Five

A small, smart office.
   *It's an outer entertaining room of the suite
of rooms belonging to the computer
components company under contract or
partly owned by* STEPHEN'*s parent
company.* FRANCES *and* STEPHEN *are
fresh from a guided tour of the factory and a
sea of young women bonding chips on to
circuit boards. They are escorted by* MR *and*
MRS LWIN, *who run the company.* MRS
LWIN *is a heavily made-up Thai lady:
European clothes with some impressive-
looking jewellery including a gold safety pin
worn as a brooch. Her husband is quite
nervous about* STEPHEN'*s visit. He doesn't
speak English at all well.* MRS LWIN *does.
There is piped music throughout like very
bad Radio One with Thai commentary but
advertising familiar products, particularly
cosmetics. We might hear mention of Max
Factor or Mary Quant.*

MRS LWIN: How is Harrods?

FRANCES: In what sense?

MRS LWIN: I've shopped there.

FRANCES: Very well, I think. I've never
shopped there.

MRS LWIN: We like England.

FRANCES: Yes?

MRS LWIN: We intend to send our son to
school in England. Have you heard of
Wolverhampton?

STEPHEN (*to* MR LWIN): The factory is
very impressive.

MR LWIN (*nodding*): Ah.

STEPHEN (*to* FRANCES): And I think
the conditions are surprisingly good.

FRANCES: Do they appreciate having the
sound system on all day?

STEPHEN: That's common all over.
English factories, the States: everywhere.

FRANCES: What are the commercials?
Are these commercials? (*Of the piped
sound.*)

MRS LWIN: For make-up, for clothes, for
aerobics. We encourage high standards of
personal appearance.

STEPHEN: They seem a contented group
of women, certainly.

MRS LWIN: Oh yes, they have good
quarters, a dormitory, with dormitory
rules so their families are happy. And
they have spending money. They can buy
motorbikes. We think it's a healthful
experience.

FRANCES: Could we call one of the girls
out and speak with her?

MRS LWIN: What do you mean?

STEPHEN: Do you mean, I don't think you
mean one of the, do you mean one of the
girls on the shop floor? I don't think
that's . . .

FRANCES: Why not? It would be nice to
hear from them how they feel.

STEPHEN: You should have asked on the
tour.

FRANCES: With the radio blaring out?
How? And anyway they're glued to their
microscopes.

MRS LWIN: Quite possible for you to do
this. Will ask Ampha. She knows some
English. (*To* STEPHEN:) Also pretty.
Won 'Guess Whose Legs These Are'
competition.

FRANCES: What?

STEPHEN: 'Guess Whose Legs These Are'
competition. They have competitions.
It's standard practice. Just fun. Yes, let's
meet Ampha.

MRS LWIN: Excuse me.

She exits. MR LWIN *uncomfortable.*

STEPHEN (*to* FRANCES): OK? Happy?

MR LWIN: Please. Sit down.

   FRANCES *does so, and* STEPHEN
reluctantly, during which FRANCES
speaks rapidly and privately to
STEPHEN.

FRANCES: Don't say it like that: OK . . .
happy . . . I couldn't work in there. Would
you let me work in there? Would you
work in there? You wouldn't.

STEPHEN (*riding over this*): Your
productivity is very good so far this year.

MR LWIN (*nodding*): Ah.

STEPHEN: The company is very pleased.
Very happy.

MR LWIN (*nodding*): Ah.

FRANCES (*privately*): Well, of course they are. Is it stupid to ask why they don't have men working here?

STEPHEN: Dexterity. The men don't have it.

MRS LWIN *returns with* AMPHA, *a factory worker in cotton worker's dress and a sunshade perhaps; so like a very down-beat croupier.*

FRANCES: I was just asking why there are no men working in the factory.

MRS LWIN: More difficult to get men. Also they get a bit bored doing same work all day. Not so peaceful as the girls.

FRANCES: Would make 'Guess Whose Legs These Are' more interesting. Hello Ampha.

AMPHA: Hello.

AMPHA'*s very shy, very reticent, anxious to please. She wears gold safety pin, very small.*

FRANCES: Do you enjoy working at Mr Lwin's factory?

AMPHA: Yes.

FRANCES: Is the pay good?

AMPHA: Oh sorry. (*Not understanding.*)

FRANCES: Is the money good?

AMPHA: Oh yes.

STEPHEN: There you are.

FRANCES (*to* STEPHEN): What else can she say? (*To* AMPHA:) Do you have any trouble with your eyes?

AMPHA: Eyes? No. No trouble.

FRANCES: Do any of the women?

STEPHEN: Frances, for goodness' sake!

AMPHA *blank.* FRANCES *looks to* MRS LWIN. *No response.*

FRANCES (*to* STEPHEN): What? (*To* AMPHA:) Are you unhappy that only women do this job? That there are only women in your factory?

AMPHA: Women very good at small things. (*Does mime of delicate manual action.*) Also bonus here for hard work: make-up, hair cut, dresses.

MRS LWIN: Not so good for men!

STEPHEN, MR, MRS LWIN *chuckle.*

FRANCES: What's your ambition, Ampha? What would you like to do in the future?

AMPHA: Understand. When stop work, want to have husband, maybe two children, one boy one girl.

FRANCES: Why when you stop work?

MRS LWIN: Company policy no married women, no children.

FRANCES (*to* STEPHEN): Is this true?

MRS LWIN: We just say marry company for few years then marry husband. Good training. Loyalty to company same thing as loyalty to husband.

FRANCES: So what happens if one of your girls gets pregnant?

MRS LWIN: Best get married, don't you think?

FRANCES: Right. Oh yes.

STEPHEN: But it's a happy factory, you would say, Ampha?

AMPHA: Very happy. Very happy factory. Thank you.

STEPHEN (*wanting this embarrassing inquisition to cease*): Fine. So then . . .

FRANCES (*dogged*): You all wear these safety pins.

MRS LWIN: Yes. Gold. Woman's club in Bangkok. Safety Pin Club. Very good.

FRANCES: Safety Pin Club? Why a safety pin?

MRS LWIN: Many reasons. Best I think is (*Unclips her safety pin.*) that point is man. (*Touches it.*) Very sharp, can be dangerous. (*Pricks herself to demonstrate.*) Hood is woman.

STEPHEN: Very clever.

FRANCES: I'll have to get my husband to buy me one, don't you think? Can I see? (MRS LWIN *shows the pin.*) I think you could say that the point is woman, very sharp, dangerous. And hood is Safety Pin Club.

MRS LWIN: Oh really? Very interesting. Will you join us now for lunch?

STEPHEN: Thank you. That's very kind, eh darling?

FRANCES: You go, Stephen.

STEPHEN: Now what? (*Mediating like crazy.*) I don't know if I said my wife is writing an article, planning to, about Bangkok, which –

FRANCES: I'm not sure I'm –

MRS LWIN: Understand. Now I understand why so many questions. Understand. (*To* MR LWIN *in Thai:*) She's writing an article. (*To* FRANCES:) Very interesting.

FRANCES: Well, then I think I'd better get back and write my article. If you'll excuse me. I can find my own way out. (*To* STEPHEN, *as she exits:*) I'll see you later tonight.

STEPHEN: After dinner?

FRANCES (*without pausing*): Unless you have further plans. In which case, fine.

STEPHEN: Right. (STEPHEN *is marooned with the* LWINS *and* AMPHA:) Yes, she writes these things.

Scene Six.
GARY's *room.*
   GARY *is propped up on the bed watching an in-hotel movie, of the Holiday Inn adult viewing variety. He's freshly laundered and has on a towelling robe. There's a knock at the door.*

GARY: Come in.

   NET *enters, with a girl,* SHEILA. *He's a little furtive.*

NET: Mr Gary, sorry disturb you.

GARY: It's all right.

NET: Here is Sheila, girlfriend for evening. All girls arrive early.

GARY: Hello Sheila.

   SHEILA *smiles.*

Is that her real name?

NET: No. But easy to say Sheila.

GARY: Suits me. Sit down Sheila. Come and sit down.

   SHEILA *smiles.*

NET: Net's problem is he arrange to take Mr Edward out this evening. Net off

duty, follow?

GARY: So what's the problem?

NET: Can you tell your friend Mr Stephen I send his girls up to room?

GARY: To his own room?

NET: No.

GARY: I was going to say: that would have been pretty dim.

NET: Not to his room. This room. This is key. (*Hands him key with room number printed on.*)

GARY: You want me to give Stephen this key? Understood.

NET: Please.

GARY: And they're up there already?

NET: Sure. Already in room.

GARY: OK.

NET: Small problem.

GARY: Which is?

NET: See, Net get this room, not official, so many things in room not working: air-conditioning, telephone . . . you follow?

GARY: Yeh.

NET: But sorry, best Net can do without more charge.

GARY: So nothing works in this room? OK. Is there a bed?

NET: Two beds. Beds no problem.

GARY: That's all right, then. Where's Edward then? Brushing his teeth?

NET: Wait for Net: reception.

GARY: Sweet.

NET: So: Net go now.

GARY: Pretty girl. Well done.

NET: No problem. Also VD card. Ask see. Very clean. Have very nice time. Nice girlfriend.

   GARY *gives* NET *a note.*

Mr Gary good friend. Net collect all girls midnight, OK?

GARY: Hey Net, leave a note at reception for Stephen to come up to me or call my room or something, otherwise time-wasting, eh?

NET: Understand.

GARY: Thought you would.

NET (*exiting*): I leave you then. Thank you.

GARY: Thanking you. (*Shutting and locking the door behind him. He surveys the room. Then he surveys SHEILA.*) I expect you've seen plenty of these before? (*The room.*) Do you speak any English? (*SHEILA shrugs.*) Doesn't matter to me. (*Looks at the floor.*) Excuse my socks. (*Gathers them up and rolls them with the discarded knickers into a ball.*) Got wet. You either get wet with sweat, don't you, or you get wet 'cause it's raining or a bit of both. Ridiculous place. Sit down. (*Pats the bed.*) Sit down. Make yourself comfortable. We can watch TV. Get a few clues, eh? You hungry? We can get food sent up. Want a hamburger? (*Blank.*) McDonalds?

SHEILA (*nods happily*): 'Donalds!

GARY (*delighted whenever they communicate*): Thought you might. We can do that. Coming up. (*He picks up phone.*) Hello. Room service? Room service? Hello? (*Speaks to SHEILA:*) I am Gary. Gary. OK? (*She nods.*) OK. (*To phone:*) Yeh. Three hamburgers please with everything on it. Yeh. Three. Uh: one seven. Thank you. That's that done. Everything is hunky dory on the hamburger front. Do you know 'How much is that Doggy in the Window?' Yeh? Well anyway it's a song. Well today we passed a hamburger shop . . . a McDonalds: understand?

SHEILA: 'Donalds!

GARY: Good! It wasn't a McDonalds, but anyway, there was this beautiful doggie. (*Does mime of dog as he explains.*) Doggie. Dog. (*Goes on to all fours, excessive impersonation.*)

SHEILA: Wo-Wo!

GARY: Right! Wo-Wo! A Wo-Wo looking at this McDonalds' window, all sad and mournful, you know, and so I thought of this great commercial they could do, you know, like (*Sings to the tune of 'How much is that Doggie in the Window?'*) 'How much is that burger in the window? . . . da dee da dee da . . . I do hope that burger's for sale!' Fab, eh?

SHEILA *chuckles.* GARY *beams.*

You like me singing, eh? What else do you like? Do you like this? (*He does a rather impressive sleight-of-hand using his lighter. The lighter apparently disappears and then GARY produces it as if from behind SHEILA's ear. She laughs. GARY finishes his magic. Stares at her as a sexual object for the first time.*) Do you have your book of, you know: the clinic thing, the VD thing? VD book? (*SHEILA nods and produces what looks like an old driving licence from her handbag. GARY gives it some scrutiny.*) Ta. How anybody's supposed to be able to read this writing! (*Referring to the Thai script:*) Legible! Right, so you're (*Very slowly:*) Khin-Thi-Da Phitpricha and you have been to the clinic every Monday and it says you were OK this week and last week and the week before and for many Mondays. Oh, see you had a small problem last year, eh? (*Points at entry in the booklet. SHEILA nods.*) Khin-Thi-Da: yeah? (*SHEILA nods.*) I am Gary. And you're . . . born (*Looks at date.*) . . . makes you: you must be seventeen. Seventeen. Khin-Thi-Da seventeen (*Counts on hand.*) Gary twenty-three (*Counts on his hands. She repeats the ages with her fingers.*) Right! Right! You seventeen: me twenty-three. Do you want to have a bath first? Eh? Bath. (*Points at bathroom. SHEILA shakes her head.*) No, not the bog . . . a bath! (*Mimes taps etc. Points at her groin.*) Give pussy a good clean, eh? A good scrub. (*Goes to bedside table and gets out his anti-biotic supplies. Continues singing his 'Burger in the Window' invention.*) See you in a minute. Ciao. (*She exits obediently.*) And I'll take a pill while we're about it.

The TV continues with its frolics and forced giggles and grey flesh. GARY settles down to watch.

Scene Seven.

NET *and* EDWARD *return to* EDWARD's *room prior to going to* NET's *cousin's house for the video.*

EDWARD (*going straight to the bathroom*): Won't be long, hang on. These bloody lenses, they're new, they're not right.

NET: No problem.

EDWARD (*off*): There are about eight different things you have to put on them. It's a complete con, Net. If I had the nerve I'd wash them in Fairy Liquid.

NET: Good boxing, eh?

EDWARD (*off*): Very interesting.

NET *does a few Thai boxing routines: a kick, a punch, etc.*

(*Off:*) Very violent.

NET: No kid?

EDWARD (*off*): No, I said, the boxing was very violent, lot of blood.

NET: See what you mean.

EDWARD (*off*): That last boy's nose was broken.

NET: Very great kick. (*Gives the bed a sample.*)

EDWARD: (*off*): What are you doing out there? Kicking my bed?

NET: Just fool around.

EDWARD (*emerging*): I've put my specs back on . . . I can't be doing with those bloody things. It's just vanity, eh?

NET: No problem.

EDWARD: Net, I don't think you really understand English. I just think you've learned some phrases like 'I understand' and 'No kid' and whatever else it is you say: 'No problem' and those are the only words you actually know. Or is that not fair?

NET: Half-half!

EDWARD: Half-half! Good! You're a bright little bugger, aren't you?

NET (*expecting to go*): OK?

EDWARD: Hang about, I can't rush in this weather. Not when it's so close. Do you want a glass of water? (*As he pours himself one.*)

NET: No.

EDWARD: What time's your cousin expecting us?

NET: No time. Any time.

EDWARD: And who's going to be there?

NET: Huh?

EDWARD: At your cousin's house . . . who will be there?

NET: Cousin. Maybe one friend, two friend, maybe wife. Maybe not expect.

EDWARD: I don't enjoy too many people at once.

NET: Understand.

EDWARD: I have enjoyed the evening so far though. Thank you.

NET (*shrugs happily*): Edward, Net's friend.

EDWARD: Net, Edward's friend.

They shake hands, comfortable then uncomfortable. A beat.

So, off tomorrow, Hong Kong.

NET: Hong Kong. Very nice?

EDWARD: No. Yes, nice place. Many problems.

NET: Chinese come in make everybody unhappy.

EDWARD: Not everybody. Not me for a kick-off. It is China anyway. Well, no actually it's Hong Kong, I mean it's not England. It's not a colony.

NET: Don't follow.

EDWARD (*looks at NET's incomprehension and laughs*): Why should Hong Kong be under anybody's foot? Britain's or China's? Like the bloody Falklands. Do you know about the Falklands?

NET: Expect so.

EDWARD: Well, it doesn't matter, Net. It's impossible. The things people have stolen. The countries countries have stolen. In my country we have a bit of Greece, a tiny bit, stone – marble – fantastic . . . and we pinched it . . . we just pinched it and we won't give it back. We were so greedy, we put it on a boat and it was so heavy the boat sank. (*Mimes.*) Lunacy. I tell you, if it could happen, if things were given back to their rightful owners - if there are natural owners, if we agree to ownership – what a bloody wind there would be, eh? The paintings and jewels and gold and stuff that would fly across the world, bloody marvellous . . . this stuff all flying home . . . And in the West, in my country . . . or in America . . . the fat that would come off! The fat that belongs to other people clawed off . . .

earrings yanked off, rings, bracelets, wallets emptied, the banks cleared, clothes stripped, every bloody thing until the skin itself would rip open and the fat and the entrails scoured until . . . until, well I'll tell you England would be stubble. The rest we pinched from somewhere. (*A beat.*) Eh? What do you think? You think shut up Edward, shut up Edward. (NET *shrugs.*) How do you think our friends are getting on?

NET: Cousin?

EDWARD: No, I mean Gary and Stephen and their girlfriends.

NET: Good time, I expect.

EDWARD: It doesn't bother you, does it?

NET: Huh?

EDWARD: It doesn't. I know. Why does it bother me that you got them girls?

NET: Edward sad maybe want girl, too?

EDWARD: No. Just something else we've stolen, isn't it? Say: 'Shut up, Edward'.

NET: Shut up, Edward.

EDWARD: You should add that to your vocabulary.

NET: Maybe go now? Net have videos.

EDWARD: What videos?

NET: Bumsin videos.

EDWARD: Blue films?

NET: Sure. Very filthy. Show everything. No kid.

EDWARD: Men and women?

NET: Boy/girl sure.

EDWARD: Always boy/girl?

NET: No. Some two girls.

EDWARD (*edgy*): Two boys?

NET: Possible. You want see two boys?

EDWARD: So easy, isn't it?

NET: Also have one video: she boys.

EDWARD: She boys? Transvestites?

NET: Kra-Toeys. (*Shrugs in amusement.*)

EDWARD: Who goes with them?

NET (*shrugs*): All crazy, you ask Net. Net drive past. Blow horn, all lift up skirts.

(*Holds his crutch to demonstrate their gesture.*) Whoo! Crazy!

EDWARD: So is everybody for sale in Bangkok?

NET: Guess so. Except maybe King.

EDWARD: So, is Net for sale?

NET (*shrugs*): Guess . . . (*Nods.*) Guess Net for sale everyday. (*He means his job.*)

EDWARD: I mean . . . as boyfriend . . .

NET: Net as boyfriend? No! (*Laughs.*) No one want Net as boyfriend! Not so pretty! Crazy.

EDWARD: What if I wanted Net as boyfriend tonight?

NET: Crazy.

EDWARD: How much?

NET (*laughs*): My friend kid Net.

EDWARD: No.

NET (*serious*): No kid?

EDWARD: No kid. How much?

NET (*shakes his head*): Edward my friend, not *boy* friend.

EDWARD: So I can't buy you?

Pause.

NET: How much you give Net?

EDWARD: How much do you want?

NET: How much you give?

EDWARD: I don't know: five hundred baht? Six hundred baht?

NET: Net find pretty boy, very cheap. Net arrange now, no problem. Very sexy.

EDWARD: A thousand baht.

NET: See, really Net not fucking boy.

EDWARD: Are you saying you want more than a thousand baht?

NET: Net unhappy.

EDWARD: Fifteen hundred baht.

NET: Fifteen hundred baht?

EDWARD: You must never say anything.

NET: For fifteen hundred baht, Net find two pretty boys. Stay all night. Do anything. No kid. Make Edward very happy. OK?

EDWARD: You don't understand, Net. You would make me very happy. I can't offer more than fifteen hundred, it's practically all the cash I have left. You can have my watch as well, if you want. Please.

NET: See, Net and Edward good friends. Problem. Net bit unhappy.

EDWARD: Edward also very unhappy. Now Net Edward's friend.

NET: Sure! very good friends!

EDWARD: I can't offer you anything else – my money and my watch. I haven't got anything else except toothbrushes.

He goes to his bed and from his pocket and wallet produces all of his cash, emptying the notes on to the bed. He throws his watch down with the money.

Sixteen hundred baht.

NET *walks slowly across to the bed, lights a cigarette. Such a lot of money.*

(Agonised, violent:) Come on! It's more than you charge for three girls!

NET *picks up the money, then the watch.*

Thank you, Net.

NET: Also toothbrushes, please.

EDWARD: What?

NET: Also toothbrushes.

EDWARD: Come on Net, they're not even really mine.

NET: Also toothbrushes.

EDWARD: OK.

NET: What you want Net to do?

EDWARD: Come here.

He beckons NET to the bed. NET dolefully walks over. Sits next to him.

(Unbuttoning NET's shirt.) I've been writing a poem about you. Take off your shirt. Take off your shirt. Somebody ruined their fingers sewing it. Take off your watch, somebody's eyes got ruined making it. Take off your jeans, take off your shirt, the cigarette is ruining you, it's killing you. (*He throws NET's cigarette into the waste bin.*) Everything we've done to you is ruining you. (*He's unzipping NET's trousers. He tries to turn him round.*) Turn round. Turn over.

The cigarette smokes from the waste bin.

Scene Eight

The coffee shop.
STEPHEN *comes out of the lift looking for a waiter.*

STEPHEN: Hello! Hello! Service!

A WAITRESS appears.

WAITRESS: Sir?

STEPHEN: I want some drinks to take up to my room.

WAITRESS (*helpfully*): Room service?

STEPHEN: Yes, I know. But the telephone's broken.

WAITRESS (*helpfully*): Can tell reception fix for you.

STEPHEN: I'm quite happy just to take the drinks up. Can you get me a drink?

WAITRESS: Sure.

STEPHEN: I want some cold beer and some coke . . . two cokes. (*Explaining.*) There's a group of us, a little party.

WAITRESS: One beer, two cokes. OK. (*Helpfully:*) Tell me room number, I tell reception fix phone.

STEPHEN: I'll do it myself. It's OK. In fact they know, actually. They know. So.

WAITRESS: You want me to take drink to room?

STEPHEN (*edgy*): No. Look, just bring the drinks here, will you, and I'll carry them up. I'm quite happy.

The WAITRESS exits. STEPHEN sits down, blows. He's very hot and flushed.
FRANCES *and* ADRIAN *emerge from the lift.*

FRANCES (*simply*): Our key's not in reception and the room's locked. I didn't know where you were or if you were back.

STEPHEN (*aggressive*): Right, I mean otherwise you wouldn't be upstairs with your chum.

FRANCES (*over this*): Otherwise I would have known where you were, Stephen. Because I thought you were staying over for dinner.

STEPHEN: I did. I thought you were going to watch Thai Boxing.

FRANCES: We decided not to go.

STEPHEN (*facetious*): Is that what you decided?

FRANCES: We went shopping for Christopher, and then we . . . anyway, I'm not going to make excuses.

ADRIAN: I said I'd come down with Frances and wait until you got back. I didn't want her to have to sit here alone.

STEPHEN: Great. Terrific. Yes, I must have gone off with the key.

FRANCES: How?

STEPHEN: I don't know. But obviously I must have as you clearly have no faults.

FRANCES: No, I just meant . . . because the key was here when I first got back. I used it. That's all I'm saying. I can't understand where it went if you haven't been . . .

STEPHEN (*pressing for the lift*): I said: I've got it. (*He reaches into his pocket. For a split second it dawns on him he has two keys. He pulls out a key and examines it as nonchalantly as he can.*) Here it is. Here is our key. Okay? (*He dangles it in front of her.*) So, I'll leave you to your little . . .

FRANCES: I'll come up with you.

STEPHEN (*presses again impatiently*): Come on, come on . . .

FRANCES: I said, I'll come with you. You don't have to stomp out.

STEPHEN: Because it's amazing isn't it? It's all fine, it's all wonderful as long as it's romantic. As long as you know the person's name before you take their pants off, that's tickety-boo. Oh yes. (*Pressing again.*) Where is this fucking lift?

ADRIAN: If Frances does go up, if you do go up, I don't want there to be any repeat of yesterday's . . .

FRANCES (*flustered*): Adrian, don't . . .

STEPHEN (*dangerous*): What's this?

ADRIAN: I think you know what I'm talking about.

STEPHEN: Oh yes: I can just imagine your little chats. About your terrible husband. Well don't bother, you know, please . . .

just . . . (*As if dismissing them.*) I've been pressing this bloody button for hours, quite astonishing.

The WAITRESS *appears with the drinks. This coincides with the lift arriving.*

WAITRESS: Want drinks downstairs now?

STEPHEN: What?

WAITRESS: Drinks.

STEPHEN: Drinks? Great. Yes. Here's fine.

FRANCES: Who are these for?

STEPHEN: Us, I suppose. There's no one else about. Thanks.

WAITRESS: Don't want in room now?

STEPHEN: No.

FRANCES: Why have you ordered coke?

STEPHEN: I want coke. Do you want coke?

FRANCES: No.

STEPHEN: Then there's beer. Adrian?

ADRIAN: No thanks.

The fire alarm sounds. Piercing noise.

FRANCES: What's going on?

ADRIAN: I don't know.

Everyone is shouting to be heard.

STEPHEN: Oh God.

ADRIAN: It's the fire alarm!

STEPHEN: What?

ADRIAN: It's the fire alarm!

The WAITRESS *rushes in, calming gestures.*

WAITRESS: Mistake. Don't worry. (*In Thai.*)

ADRIAN: What?

WAITRESS: Mistake. Mistake. Don't worry. (*In Thai.*)

FRANCES: What's she saying?

ADRIAN: I don't know.

GARY *rushes in with* SHEILA, *they're in towelling dressing gowns.*

GARY: What's going on?

ADRIAN: Is there smoke upstairs?

GARY: I don't know. I thought I could smell smoke.

The WAITRESS *talks in Thai to* SHEILA.

(*To* SHEILA): What's she saying?

WAITRESS: No problem.

GARY (*to* STEPHEN): Where are your two?

STEPHEN *not responding.*

Stephen! Where are your two? Fucking hell!

STEPHEN *sits down.*

Are they still upstairs? Christ? Where's the key? The key! (*He shakes* STEPHEN *and pulls the key from his grasp.*)

FRANCES: What's going on?

GARY: Ask him! (*He rushes out.* SHEILA *tries to stop him.*)

FRANCES: Stephen!

ADRIAN: We should go outside, just in case. Let's go to the pool. Frances . . .

FRANCES: Stephen, come on.

ADRIAN (*to the* WAITRESS *and to* SHEILA): Come on. (*He pulls them towards the exterior exit. They exit.*)

FRANCES *pulls* STEPHEN *up.* EDWARD *and* NET *come in, both dishevelled.*

NET (*shouting*): No problem! Stop! False 'larm! False 'larm!

The alarm ceases as abruptly as it began. NET *and* EDWARD *speak absolutely simultaneously.*

False 'larm. Sorry. No problem. Net have cigarette, set fire to bin. Small fire. No problem.

ADRIAN: What? You mean . . . ?

EDWARD: Yes, we were in my room. There was an accident with a cigarette. The rubbish bin caught fire. We didn't notice, and then there was a lot of smoke and it set the thing off.

NET: Every week fire alarm. Nobody else pay too much attention.

FRANCES: Stephen, what's going on? Where did Gary go? Stephen? (*To* ADRIAN:) I don't know what's . . .

(*Frowns at* STEPHEN.)

ADRIAN (*to* EDWARD *of his explanation*): Bit odd, isn't it?

EDWARD: What's odd?

ADRIAN: Not noticing that the bin was on fire.

EDWARD (*violently*): No. And we did notice eventually, but by then it was too late. What are you trying to say?

ADRIAN: I was just asking a question.

EDWARD: No, come on, come on, I'm not having you just, I can't stand it when people make a remark and then just –

EDWARD *is interrupted by the lift suddenly spilling open to reveal* GARY *with the two girls, one wrapped in a sheet, the other in a towel. One of them still has a ripped and knotted sheet dragging around her ankle and wrist. Both of them are pretty shaken-up.*

GARY (*quiet, disgusted*): He'd tied them to the bed. These two women. They were naked and tied to the bed. They couldn't move. Do you believe that? He just left them. If there had have been a real fire, they would have burned to death.

He throws the hotel key at STEPHEN's *feet.*

Scene Nine.

Outside the hotel. Morning.
NET *appears.burdened by as much luggage as he can manage. It's all clearly labelled with Eastern Promise tags. He dumps his load as* EDWARD *appears carrying a flight bag and a paper package.* NET *immediately walks past* EDWARD, *without acknowledging him.*

EDWARD: Net . . .

NET *stops, but doesn't turn around.*

Net, I've wrapped, I've put the toothbrushes in this . . . you didn't take them last night in all the, but anyway, I hope you get a good . . .

NET *turns, but without warmth.*

NET (*refusing*): Take toothbrush Hong Kong. Best thing. Net have toothbrush already.

EDWARD: No, they're yours.

NET: OK, Net give toothbrush Hong Kong.

EDWARD: Then I'll send you money.

NET: No.

EDWARD: I haven't slept.

NET: No kid?

EDWARD: No kid.

NET: Big storm.

EDWARD: Buddha taking bath . . . isn't that what you say? (NET *shrugs*.) Anyway, the rain's good, it – I think – it's I was going to say it cleanses, it feels cleaner this morning, but that's a bit obvious, isn't it? Net, I'd like to take a photograph of you.

NET: No.

EDWARD: Please.

NET: No.

EDWARD *raises camera*. NET *turns his back*.

EDWARD: Please Net, turn around.

NET: No, don't want turn around.

EDWARD: I'll take the picture, anyway.

No effect. NET *keeps his back turned.* EDWARD *takes a photograph of the back of his head.*

Well. (NET *still facing away*.) How's the watch? Are you pleased with it?

NET: Sure.

EDWARD: I'm happy you're wearing my watch.

NET: May sell sometime. Who knows?

EDWARD: Net, I wanted to explain about last night, before I go – I'd like to write to you anyway –

FRANCES *and* STEPHEN *enter with their hand luggage.* EDWARD *recovers himself.*

FRANCES: Hello.

EDWARD: Good morning.

NET: Morning.

FRANCES: Has anyone turned up yet, do you know?

EDWARD: No. It's early yet, I think. And I expect Net will be driving us to the airport? Yes?

NET: No. (*To* FRANCES:) What you want? Eastern Promise Tour Rep?

FRANCES: No rush.

NET: Net go look: no problem.

EDWARD: Net. Net.

NET *exits. The others stand uncomfortably, subdued.*

FRANCES: Will it be raining in Hong Kong, do you think?

EDWARD: Expect so.

FRANCES: Do you always do this? Stop off in Bangkok?

EDWARD: Have done, yes.

FRANCES: Does it repay more than one visit?

Enter GARY and ADRIAN with bags.

Hello.

ADRIAN: Hello.

GARY (*to* FRANCES): How's the psychopath?

FRANCES *ignores him.*

(*To* STEPHEN:) Questions have to be asked about you, mate. Something of a struggle on the old pervert front. (*With some feeling:*) How can you stay with him? No, really. I'm fascinated.

ADRIAN: Shut up Gary.

GARY: Certainly sir. (*To* EDWARD:) And what about your little friend? Has he lubricated the front step this morning?

EDWARD: I've seen him, yes.

GARY: Little twat owes me some money.

EDWARD: Net does?

GARY: And I intend to get it off him before we go. 'Cause I got ripped off last night, in all the commotion, didn't I? Lost my watch, which was not a cheap watch, and some cash. Bitch had it away, didn't she? It's a fucking rip-off, this place.

ADRIAN: Gary, I suggest you shut your mouth.

GARY: Why should I?

ADRIAN: Well let's start with Jeannie, shall we?

GARY: What?

ADRIAN: Because she's going to be very interested in what we did on our holidays, isn't she?

EDWARD: I can write you a cheque if Net owes you money, although I can't quite see that he does.

ADRIAN (*over this*): He'll survive.

Horn sounds.

FRANCES (*to* ADRIAN): Is this us?

ADRIAN: It's you, I think, probably.

FRANCES: What does that mean?

ADRIAN: Gary and I are going back to London, or rather we're going to sign a contract this morning – we're getting a taxi – and then we're going back to London.

FRANCES: What about Hong Kong? Are you joking?

The TOUR OPERATOR *appears: smart, efficient and late. She reads from her clipboard.*

TOUR OPERATOR: Ah, Mr, Mrs Britter, Mr West, Mr Alexander, Mr Gover, please board bus, have all bags ready and check have ticket and passport before leaving hotel. Also check you have no bill outstanding at the hotel of your stay. Hurry please, thank you.

ADRIAN (*to the* TOUR OPERATOR): Well, actually, yes, I rang your company yesterday and explained that we were, this is Mr West and Mr Alexander, I explained that we were returning to London and . . .

TOUR OPERATOR: Sure, OK, no problem, I remember, I have written down somewhere. (*Searches through her clipboard.*) OK, everyone on bus please.

NET *has appeared with the rest of the luggage and now begins to move it in the direction of the bus.*

GARY: Not ours. (*Of the luggage.*)

EDWARD: Net!

GARY: And where's my watch?

EDWARD: Net, I can carry my own case.

NET, *head down, pushes off the Britters' luggage. Perhaps exchanges a monosyllabic word or two with the courier in Thai. During this:*

FRANCES: Yesterday?

ADRIAN: Yesterday what?

FRANCES: You changed your plans yesterday?

ADRIAN: Yes.

FRANCES: I don't want to be completely uh, but what time yesterday? No, don't answer that. (*To* STEPHEN:) We should go.

TOUR OPERATOR (*exiting*): Hurry please.

NET *has taken all the Hong Kong luggage. He returns and approaches* ADRIAN.

NET: You want taxi, sir?

ADRIAN: Please.

EDWARD: Net, I have to go.

GARY: Is he going to answer me about that watch?

EDWARD: Will you shut up about your bloody watch! (*To* NET:) He says he had his watch stolen last night.

The horn, insistent.

STEPHEN: I'll see you in the bus. (*He exits.*)

FRANCES: No, I'm coming now.

NET (*taking off the watch* EDWARD *has given him*): No problem: have Net's watch.

EDWARD: No!

GARY (*dropping it casually*): I don't want your crappy watch. I want my own.

NET *exits, angrily, back to the hotel.*

Oy! Where you going? What about our cab?

EDWARD: Net! (*Rounds on* GARY:) You're rubbish, aren't you?

GARY (*dangerous*): Be careful, lovey.

ADRIAN (*defusing the argument*): Gary, go and find a cab then.

GARY (*to* FRANCES): You should come back with us. Look what you're left with.

Come back with us. (*Exits.*)

EDWARD, ADRIAN *and* FRANCES
stand in silence. EDWARD *realises
they're waiting for him to go.*

EDWARD: I'll say goodbye, then.

ADRIAN: Right.

EDWARD *exits.*

You could come back with us.

FRANCES: How could I? Do you want me
to? Tell me. (*She waits for something
from him. It doesn't come.*) Yes, I can see
I'm a liability.

ADRIAN: No, I think you're great.

FRANCES: Oh yes, but not irresistibly
great. That's the problem.

ADRIAN: I bought you these. (*Producing
a small jewellery box.*) They're sapphires.
I had an address. Supposed to be quite
good.

FRANCES: My ears aren't pierced.

ADRIAN: Well, now's your chance.

FRANCES: To have them done? No, I
don't think so. I've survived this long.
(*The horn again, insistent.* FRANCES *is
suddenly bleak:*) How can I stay with
him? How can I? (*A beat, then
recovering:*) I hate this kind of weather so
much.

STEPHEN *reappears.*

STEPHEN (*of the minibus*): If you don't
come now, I think we'll . . .

FRANCES (*cutting him off*): Right.

STEPHEN *stops, looks at them, then
turns and exits.*

(*To* ADRIAN:) I'll see you, then.

ADRIAN: No, you won't, Frances.

FRANCES: No, that's right. Goodbye,
then.

ADRIAN: Goodbye.

They turn and exit in opposite directions.

Scene Ten

GARY'*s bedroom.*
*Two chambermaids enter. They set about
stripping the bed and changing the sheets and*
renewing the bathroom linen. One of them
turns on the wireless which is pumping out
Thai music and a Thai DJ. They change the
sheets in an elegant, practised way and are
perfectly at ease. If the actresses are
themselves Thai speakers let them chat idly
under the volume of the music. In any case
they can laugh and enjoy each other's
company and be familiar with the music and
react, comprehending, to the words of the
DJ.*

In the process, one of them comes across
GARY's *watch. It spills on to the floor. She
picks it up and she and her friend discuss it.
She laughs and pockets it.*

*They roll up the soiled linen and replace it
with large, pristine white sheets. Suddenly
everything is white. The girls exit.*